The Essential
Catholic Prayer Book

The Essential Catholic Prayer Book

A COLLECTION OF PRIVATE AND COMMUNITY PRAYERS

With a Glossary of Key Terms and
a Brief Manual of Ways to Pray

A REDEMPTORIST PASTORAL PUBLICATION

Liguori
LIGUORI, MISSOURI

Imprimi Potest:
Richard Thibodeau, C.Ss.R.
Provincial, Denver Province
The Redemptorists

Published by Liguori Publications
Liguori, Missouri
www.liguori.org
www.catholicbooksonline.com

Library of Congress Cataloging-in-Publication Data

Bauer, Judith A.
    The essential Catholic prayer book : a collection of private and community prayers : with a glossary of key terms and a brief manual of ways to pray / edited and compiled by Judith A. Bauer. — 1st ed.
       p.   cm. — (A Redemptorist pastoral publication)
    ISBN 0-7648-0488-X (pbk.)
    1. Catholic Church Prayer-books and devotions—English. I. Bauer, Judy, 1941– . II. Series.
BX2110.E77 1999
242'.802—dc21   99-40997

Contents

Contents

Contents

Contents

Section Seven
Prayers to the Blessed Virgin Mary 115

Contents

Introduction

The stressful and threatening events of our day can only be faced with equilibrium by people who pray. Without prayer, our faith grows cold, our love is misdirected, and our hope becomes a shaky matter at best. Prayer should be a daily event, not just a Sundays-only effort.

While the liturgical celebration of the holy sacrifice of the Mass is the summit of prayer for those called to the lay vocation, all agree with the Second Vatican Council which says the following in its Constitution on the Sacred Liturgy:

> The spiritual life, however, is not limited solely to participation in the liturgy. The Christian is indeed called to pray to his Father in secret; furthermore, according to the teaching of the Apostle, he must pray without ceasing (§12).

Thus, this small book is presented in hopes of providing three things: (1) a collection of basic Catholic prayers that will gather in one place a wealth of prayers and devotions, traditional as well as new, that cover a wide range of needs and circumstances; (2) basic information on prayer types and strategies that will give readers a central source for learning about the prayer traditions of the Church, and perhaps give them insight to different ways to pray that might refresh and reinvigorate a life of prayer; and (3) fundamental definitions and explanations about praying and prayer that may be used as a reference, as part of a group learning experience, or for self-study.

Section One, "Prayer: Into the Arms of God," presents a brief introduction to prayer and its place in our life of faith. Sections Two is a compilation of everyday, basic prayers for morning, daytime, and evening, including those prayers familiar to almost every Catholic.

Section Three compiles prayers and information that center around the holy sacrifice of the Mass. This includes an explanation of the order of the Mass, including some of the most familiar Mass prayers, prayers before and after Mass, as well as prayers before and after holy Communion.

Section Four centers on the sacrament of penance, presenting prayers suitable for saying before and after confession as well as a description of the Order of Individual Confession.

Section Five draws together prayers addressed to Jesus Christ. Here the reader will also find the Stations of the Cross, prayers to the Sacred Heart and Precious Blood of Christ, as well as prayers devoted to the Holy Name and the Child Jesus. At the end of this section are prayers in honor of the Divine Mercy and the Holy Eucharist.

Section Six includes prayers to the Holy Spirit and the Blessed Trinity, while Section Seven collects prayers and devotions to the Blessed Virgin Mary.

Section Eight offers prayers suitable for personal needs; and Section Nine compiles seven complete prayers services aimed primarily at home celebrations that can be observed over the course of the Church year.

Section Ten is a treasury of prayers for the sick, the dying, and the deceased, including the souls in purgatory; and Section Eleven brings together prayers to the angels and saints, including Saint Joseph. Section Twelve collects prayers for friends, family, and special intentions. Section Thirteen offers differing ways to pray and includes suggestions and some recommended sources as well. And, finally, Section Fourteen is a glossary of significant prayer-related terms presented in an easy-to-read format along with pronunciation guides for unfamiliar words.

It is our hope that no matter how you chose to use this volume, you will find it an invaluable resource for expanding and enlarging your prayer life.

BROTHER DAN KORN, C.SS.R.
Liguori Publications
Feast of Anthony of Padua
JUNE 13, 1999

Prayer:
In the Arms of God

1. What Is Prayer?

The *Catechism of the Catholic Church* gives a very beautiful definition of prayer from Saint Thérèse of Lisieux. She says that prayer is a "surge of the heart," a look toward heaven, a "cry of recognition and love, embracing both trial and joy" (*CCC* §2558). The *Catechism* also gives other definitions: "Prayer is the raising of one's mind and heart to God" (*CCC* §2559) and a "response of faith to the free promise of salvation" (*CCC* §2561).

There are probably as many definitions of prayer as there are people who write about it. Saint Augustine says that prayer is "nothing but love." Poet George Herbert (d. 1633) calls prayer "Christ's banquet," "God's breath in man," and the "heart's pilgrimage." Thomas Merton describes prayer in this way:

> Prayer is freedom and affirmation growing out of nothingness into love. Prayer is the flowing of our innermost freedom, in response to the word of God. Prayer is not only dialogue with God: it is the communion of our freedom with his ultimate freedom, His infinite Spirit.

The *Catechism* goes on to tell us more about prayer: (1) Prayer is a gift of God, the loving response of human beings to "God's desire for us" (*CCC* §§2559, 2560); (2) Prayer is a covenant and compact between human beings and God in Jesus Christ (*CCC* §2564); (3) Prayer is seated in the heart but it is the whole person who prays (*CCC* §2562); (4) Prayer is the loving interaction of God's children with the Father, Son, and Holy Spirit—the Trinity (*CCC* §2525); and (5) Prayer is a habit of resting in the presence of the triune God (*CCC* §2565).

Even seen in its human framework (certainly prayer is a sign of our humanity), prayer is a great mystery. God requests our attention in prayer; he calls us tirelessly to prayer even though we are sinners.

Psalm 139 (138) points out that we cannot escape the Lord. It says: "Where else could I go from your Spirit? Where could I flee from your presence?" (Ps 139:7).

2. Why Do We Pray?

We pray in answer to God's call and as a consequence of our status as beings of his creation. He has called us from nothingness into existence, and he continues to call us to be his children. We are made in his likeness and thus we have embedded in us the need, the desire, the impulse to praise him for all the majestic wonders he has created and for the gift of our own salvation.

We may forget our Creator or follow after false idols or accuse him of deserting us, but our true God relentlessly summons us and reveals himself to us throughout the whole of salvation history. We pray in response to the presence and action of God in our world.

We pray because we believe; we pray as a response of faith to the reality of God's existence in our lives. Prayer also expresses our earnest hope, our firm stance, that our salvation is at hand, that Christ will indeed return on the last day. Prayer fills us with the Holy Spirit who brings us an abundance of hope, joy, and peace. We pray because we are in love with Christ and wish to respond by loving him as he has loved us in his dying for us. Love, says the *Catechism*, is the "source and summit of prayer" (*CCC* §2658).

3. How Is Prayer Modeled in the Old Testament?

The drama of prayer is revealed to us in the Old Testament and is identified most often with the intimate personal contact of God with his people. At the beginning, the first great prophet of prayer was Abraham, who submissively answered God's call, going off to a strange land, building an altar to the Lord at each stage of his journey. Abraham's first prayer was a prayer of faith, tested by action. His prayer was silent, marked not by words but by "attentiveness of the

3

heart" (*CCC* §2570). As time went on, Abraham became more comfortable with God's promises and he welcomed God as a guest at Mamre. Then, with even greater confidence, he interceded with God for the doomed cities of Sodom and Gomorrah (though his intercession does not succeed). Finally, God confronts Abraham with his biggest test of faith, a request to sacrifice the son God had given him. Faithfully, Abraham followed God's instructions, realizing that all things were possible to God. In the end, God intervened, providing another sacrifice in place of Abraham's son, Isaac. In all these events, Abraham demonstrates an important aspect of prayer. He *lived* his faith; his prayer took the form of action.

Later in the Old Testament, Moses would be called by God from the midst of a burning bush, which would become a fiery prototype of God's call to us to pray and a signifier of a holy place to worship. Moses eventually becomes God's messenger and leads the Israelites from Egypt. Moses models prayer as a holy friendship, of one man speaking to his friend, face to face, and as the *Catechism* says, in this relationship Moses reveals the characteristic of contemplative prayer (*CCC* §2576). Moses' intimacy with God as God's prophet and messenger and his role as mediator between God and his people who have fallen victim to idolatry shows his great determination to fulfill the word of God.

David, a king "after God's own heart," is another example of the human experience of prayer. At the dedication of the Temple, David raises his hands to heaven and pleads with the Lord, for himself and for his people, to forgive their sins and to provide for their daily needs, so that all nations may know that there is only one God Most High and that the worship of his people may belong entirely to him (*CCC* §2580).

David's people went on to use the Temple as a school of prayer where they would offer sacrifices, incense, and other signs of the holiness of God. But this prayer became hollow and ritualistic, so

God sent Elijah, the father of the prophets, to show the power and effectiveness of the prayer of the righteous.

Through the miraculous multiplication of the flour and oil, Elijah shows the widow of Zarephath that the promises of the Lord will be fulfilled; and through Elijah's pleading prayer on behalf of the widow's son, God brings the boy back to life.

In addition to the instances of individual prayer, the Old Testament tells of the important role prayer plays in the life of the people of Israel. Indeed, from them we receive that masterpiece of prayer, the Book of Psalms, or the Psalter. Saint Ambrose describes them beautifully:

> What is more pleasing than a psalm? David expresses it well: "Praise the Lord, for a psalm is good: let there be praise of our God with gladness and grace!" Yes, a psalm is a blessing on the lips of the people, praise of God, praise of God, …the voice of the Church, a confession of faith in song (*CCC* §2589).

The psalms present two kinds of prayer, the personal and the communal. Besides telling the history of God's people, the psalms reflect the varied human experiences of those who composed them. There is a simplicity and a spontaneity about these songs of Israel. They reflect the full gamut of human prayer and emotion: praise, thanks, fear, exultation, depression, anger, sorrow, joy.

4. How Is Prayer Taught in the New Testament?

The Gospels tell us how Jesus prayed and how he taught us to pray. In Luke, for example, Jesus is portrayed as going off to a quiet place to pray, often spending the whole night in prayer and in wordless communion with his Father. The *Catechism* says: "He includes all men in his prayer, for he has taken on humanity in his incarnation, and he offers [us] to the Father when he offers himself" (*CCC* §2602).

Before deciding moments in his life and his mission, Jesus is found in prayer: at his baptism, his call of the Twelve, his transfiguration, his passion.

Luke 11:1 gives a moving picture of Jesus at prayer: Jesus "was praying in a certain place and when he had finished, one of his disciples said to him, 'Lord, teach us to pray....'" Notice that the disciples are impressed with seeing Jesus so deeply absorbed, and they want to experience what is so apparent in Jesus' prayer.

Yet, not all of Jesus' prayers were joyful. There were also the prayers of his passion. The Letter to the Hebrews reminds us that Christ, "in the days of his mortal life, offered his sacrifice with tears and cries. He prayed to him who could save him from death...."

Jesus took very seriously the disciples' request to be taught about prayer. He entrusted to them and to his Church the most essential Christian prayer: the seven petitions of the Our Father—a summary of the whole gospel, the centerpiece of the Scriptures, and the most perfect of all prayers. Saint Augustine says so aptly in his *Epistulae*:

> Run through all the words of the holy prayers [in Scripture], and I do not think that you will find anything in them that is not contained and included in the Lord's Prayer.

Central to Jesus' teaching about prayer was an emphasis on conversion of heart. As the *Catechism* says, "If our heart is far from God, the words of prayer are in vain" (*CCC* §2562). Reconciliation with one's brothers and sisters, love of enemies and prayer for persecutors, prayer in secret, and prayer of forgiveness are all essential preliminaries to effective prayer.

Jesus also asked that those who pray keep attentive and faithful watch, that they pray urgently and without ceasing, that their hearts be humble as was that of the tax collector, and that they "ask in his name" (Jn 14:13).

The New Testament also tells us of the prayer of Mary, the Mother of Jesus: her unconditional surrender of faith to the role God calls her to perform in the drama of salvation. There is also her bold prayer in the *Magnificat* for a new world in which false values would be overturned and the mighty overthrown. God's poor would inherit the kingdom of God and peace and justice would reign on the earth (*CCC* §2598–2622).

5. How Should We Pray?

Prayer is something personal and varied. There are no recipes or magic formulas for praying. But the New Testament tells us one thing: "When you pray, do not use a lot of words, as the pagans do, for they hold that the more they say, the more chance they have of being heard. Do not be like them" (Mt 6:7–8).

Prayer can be very serious and sober; prayer can also be filled with laughter. Prayer can consist in pouring out our heart before God, in lamenting and sorrow. Prayer can be made up of confession and shame and of surrender to God's will. Prayer can consist of *praise*, which sings God's glory, not for what God has done but for who he is; *thanksgiving,* which celebrates the wonders God has wrought for us in creation and even more miraculously in his work of salvation; *petition*, which is prayer that acknowledges our status as creatures and our total dependence on God; *intercession*, which is prayer on behalf of others that signifies our awareness of communion with all God's people. It makes us realize that we are a communion of saints who journey together toward God.

The ways of prayer can also be distinguished. There is *vocal prayer* which can happen spontaneously, but which also can adhere to set words. This prayer can take place quietly in one's room, or in community, whether in groups, in the family, or in the public liturgy. Vocal prayer also includes the rhythmic repetition of certain forms, such as the rosary or the Jesus Prayer.

Beyond vocal prayer is *meditative prayer*, which is above all a quest to discover what God wants of us and what response we need to make to the divine will. Meditative prayer is sometimes facilitated by the pondering of a text, especially ones from Scripture, the liturgy, or the works of the great spiritual writers. Meditation is not made up of clever thoughts or overwhelming pieces of information. These things do not give the soul its fill. Only attentiveness to God and willingness to imitate Christ lead us to a feeling of completeness in prayer.

On another level beyond meditative prayer is *prayer of the heart* or *contemplation*. This prayer is a gift from God in which one becomes wordlessly aware of the presence of God and a union with him. The mystics often experienced this kind of prayer.

All these definitions and distinctions should not obscure the fact that prayer is a simple matter. Pope John Paul II gives this advice:

Pray any way you like, so long as you do pray. Say prayers that your mother taught you. Pray any way you like, but you must pray.

And never say: "I don't pray because I don't know how to pray!" because this simply isn't true. Everyone knows how to pray. The words of prayer are simple and the rest follows.

To say "I don't know how to pray" means that you are deceiving yourself. Yourself and who else? Who can you deceive about this? It always means some smallness of heart. Some lack of good will. Or sometimes of courage. It is possible to pray, and necessary to pray.

Pray any way you like. From a book or from memory, it's all the same. Maybe just in thought. A person can pray perfectly when, for example, he is out on the hills or on a lake and he feels at one with nature. Nature speaks for him or rather speaks to him. He prays perfectly (John Paul II).

6. How Should We Overcome Difficulties in Prayer?

The Christian life is a struggle to live the demands of the gospel. Our prayer life reflects that struggle. The *Catechism* says, "We pray as we live, because we live as we pray" (*CCC* §2725). Prayer is not just a sudden impulse that overtakes us; it is a commitment.

A common problem of prayer is distraction. Our lives are busy, noisy, and stressful. To deal with distractions in prayer, we need to deal with our lifestyle. If we live frantic lives, our prayer will be equally distracted. We pray as we live.

Still, we should not become overly anxious about the issue of distractions. To some degree, distractions are inevitable. What is important, above all, is daily faithfulness to prayer.

Perhaps it is important to recall Paul's words: "We are weak, but the Spirit comes to help us. How to ask? And what shall we ask for? We do not know, but the spirit intercedes for us without words" (Rom 8:26).

Another common problem is wounded pride, hardened by our not being heard according to our own will or disappointed by our failure to achieve our own goals instead of God's goals. To overcome this difficulty requires vigilance, an understanding that Jesus is coming not only on the last day but every day.

Sometimes difficulty in prayer arises out of our faulty sense of entitlement when we intercede for ourselves or others and claim that God has not heard our prayers. Since God has not responded as we wish, then the temptation is to stop praying. However, God hears and answers every prayer, knowing the future and what is best for us. Besides, our prayer should be focused on God, who gives, and not on *what* God gives. As the *Catechism* teaches, Christ prays for us, in our place and on our behalf (*CCC* §2740). He never stops interceding for us with the Father who will hear his prayer when we pray faithfully.

Another prayer difficulty is termed *dryness*. It is a moment when the person at prayer is without spiritual comfort. This feeling of desertion should be countered by "sheer faith clinging faithfully to Jesus in his agony and in his tomb" (*CCC* §2731).

Another hindrance to prayer can be a sort of spiritual depression called *acedia*. It arises from a certain laxness and carelessness of the heart and from overindulgence in the flesh. Humility is the painful prescription for this depression, an acceptance of any discouragement that only leads the humble spirit to trust more in the love of God.

SECTION TWO

Prayers for Everyday

1. Basic Prayers

SIGN OF THE CROSS

This prayer, combined with the sign of the Cross, serves as the beginning and conclusion of every prayer and action. It sanctifies our lives in conse-cration to the three persons of the Blessed Trinity.

In the name of the Father, and of the Son, and of the Holy Spirit. Amen.

THE GLORY BE (OR THE DOXOLOGY)

A profession in praise of the Blessed Trinity, this prayer has been in use since the early days of the Church.

Glory be to the Father, and to the Son, and to the Holy Spirit. As it was in the beginning, is now, and ever shall be, world without end. Amen.

THE OUR FATHER (OR THE LORD'S PRAYER)

In response to the request of the disciples that Our Lord teach them how to pray, Jesus gives them the Our Father, truly a summary of the gospel and at the center of the Scriptures (CCC §2773–2774).

Our Father, who art in heaven, hallowed by thy name; the king-dom come; thy will be done on earth as it is in heaven. Give us this day our daily bread; and forgive us our trespasses as we forgive those who trespass against us; and lead us not into temptation, but deliver us from evil. Amen.

HAIL MARY (OR *AVE MARIA*)

This prayer is formally called the "Angelic Salutation" since it is based on a passage from the Gospel of Luke which contains the first line of the prayer. By the beginning of the twelfth century, the first part of the prayer was in common use in the liturgy of the West. The second part of the prayer beginning "Holy Mary" was added about the fifteenth century.

Hail Mary, full of grace! The Lord is with you; blessed are you among women, and blessed is the fruit of your womb, Jesus. Holy Mary, Mother of God, pray for us sinners, now and at the hour of our death. Amen.

THE APOSTLES' CREED

This prayer is an ancient creed used at baptisms in the early Roman Church. It is called the Apostles' Creed because it is thought to be a summary of the teachings of the apostles.

I believe in God, the Father almighty, creator of heaven and earth.

I believe in Jesus Christ, his only Son, our Lord. He was conceived by the power of the Holy Spirit and born of the Virgin Mary. He suffered under Pontius Pilate, was crucified, died, and was buried. He descended into hell. On the third day he rose again. He ascended into heaven, and is seated at the right hand of the Father. He will come again to judge the living and the dead.

I believe in the Holy Spirit, the holy Catholic Church, the communion of saints, the forgiveness of sins, the resurrection of the body, and life everlasting. Amen.

ACT OF FAITH

O my God, I firmly believe that you are one God in three divine Persons, Father, Son, and Holy Spirit; I believe that your divine Son became man and died for our sins, and that he shall come to judge the living and the dead. I believe these and all the truths that the holy Catholic Church teaches, because you have revealed them, who can neither deceive nor be deceived. Amen.

ACT OF HOPE

O my God, relying on your almighty power and infinite mercy and promises, I hope to obtain pardon for my sins, the help of your grace, and life everlasting, through the merits of Jesus Christ, my Lord and Redeemer. Amen.

ACT OF LOVE

O my God, I love you above all things, with my whole heart and soul, because you are all-good and worthy of all love. I love my neighbor as myself for the love of you. I forgive all who have injured me and ask pardon of all whom I have injured. Amen.

ACT OF CONTRITION

O my God, I am heartily sorry for all my sins. In choosing to do wrong and failing to do good, I have sinned against you whom I should love above all things. I firmly intend, with your help, to do penance, to sin no more, and to avoid whatever leads me to sin. Our Savior Jesus Christ suffered and died for us. In his name, my God, have mercy. Amen.

PRAYER FOR THE POPE

Lord Jesus Christ, you granted to Peter and his successors the power to exercise your authority over the flock which is your Church. Grant to our Holy Father the grace to follow your will in all things, the courage to protect your Church from all threats, and holiness to be an example to all humankind. Help him as he works in unity with the other bishops as priest, teacher, and shepherd. Preserve him and give him the joy of seeing the Church grow in strength and in grace. Amen.

2. Morning Prayers

MORNING OFFERING

O Jesus, through the Immaculate Heart of your mother, Mary, I offer you today my prayers, my sufferings, my disappointments, my joys, and all my works. I give you these together with all that is offered to you in the sacrifice of the Mass everywhere in the world. I give this gift today in reparation for my sins, for the needs of people throughout the world, for the intentions and needs of my loved ones, and for our Holy Father. Amen.

LET US AWAKE

The whole world is asleep, and God so full of goodness, so great, so worthy of all praise, no one is thinking of Him! See, nature praises Him, and man...who ought to praise Him, sleeps! Let us go, let us go and wake the universe...and sing His praises!

BLESSED MARIAM BAOUARDY

O LORD, MY STRENGTH

I love you, Lord, my strength, my fortress, my savior. While I lay asleep, you held me in your hands: stand by me and shield me while I am awake. Let your good Spirit guide me in ways that are level and smooth. O God, you are my God, my happiness lies in you alone.

Glory be to God the Father, who has chosen us in Christ to be his adopted children.

Glory be to God the Son, our Lord and Savior Jesus Christ, through whose blood we have gained our freedom.

Glory be to God the Holy Spirit, living in us, the pledge of our inheritance, the seal with which we have been stamped. Amen.

PRAYER TO ONE'S GUARDIAN ANGEL

My Guardian Angel, God has sent you to me to guide me; I am in your care. Be my constant companion and protect me throughout this day. Do not let me go astray and warn me of every danger to both body and soul. Amen.

PRAYER FOR THE DAY'S ACTIVITIES

Give me, dear Lord, a pure heart and a wise mind, that I may carry out my work according to your will. Save me from all false desires, from pride, greed, envy, and anger, and let me accept joyfully every task you set before me. Let me seek to serve the poor, the sad, and those unable to work. Help me to discern honestly my own gifts that I may do the things of which I am capable, and happily and humbly leave the rest to others. Above all, remind me constantly that I have nothing except what you give me, and can do nothing except what you enable me to do.

JACOB BOEHME

PSALM 95 (94)

This hymn of praise to God began the Sabbath liturgy of the Jewish people. It is now said at the beginning of each day's Liturgy of the Hours. Saying this morning prayer unites one's intentions more closely to the common prayer of the Church.

> Come, let us sing to the Lord,
> let us make a joyful sound
> to the Rock of our salvation.
> Let us come before him giving thanks,
> with music and songs of praise.
> For the Lord is the great God,
> the great King above all gods.

In his hand are the depths of the earth
and the mountain heights.
The sea is his, for he made it,
and his hand shaped the dry land.
Come and worship; let us bow down,
kneel before the Lord, our Maker.
He is our God, and we his people;
the flock he leads and pastures.

PRAYER TO UNITE WITH GOD'S WILL

My God, I do not know what may happen to me this day; but of one thing I am certain: that nothing will happen but what you have foreseen and ordered from all eternity. I submit myself to your eternal plan and accept it with a willing heart. I unite myself to the sacrifice of Jesus Christ, my Savior. In his name, and through his merits, I ask of you patience in all my trials and disappointments, and a total submission to all that will happen to me according to your divine plan. Amen.

PRAYER FOR GUIDANCE

Almighty God, as the earth awakes to a new day, I offer you whatever will grow, increase, and multiply this day and also what will diminish and die: life and death, joys and hopes of all people everywhere, their tears and their sweat, and also my own. I hold them all up to you in union with Christ and through him. May your blessing descend upon the earth, heal the wounds opened by sin, and make of all peoples a family, no longer ruled by power and violence, but by love, justice, and peace.

Make me an instrument of your peace. Give me a generous heart, never paying back one wrong with another, an angry word with another, but always paying back with a blessing.

Fill my heart with your love. Keep me in the good will of my friends. Correct my defects and give strength to my good qualities.

Make me honest and kind, patient and reliable, helpful to all. Bless my family and my dear ones, and keep them in your loving care. Amen.

CANTICLE OF ZACHARY

At daybreak the Church sings the declaration of faith made by the father of John the Baptist, the precursor of Christ. As the rising sun colors the sky, so he came to lighten our darkness.

Blessed be the Lord, the God of Israel; he has visited his people and wrought their redemption.

He has raised up a scepter of salvation for us, among the posterity of his servant David,

According to the promise which he made by the lips of holy men that have been his prophets from the beginning;

Salvation from our enemies, and from the hand of all those who hate us.

So he would carry out his merciful design toward our fathers, by remembering his holy covenant.

He had sworn an oath to our Father Abraham, that he would enable us to live without fear in his service.

Delivered from the hand of our enemies,

Passing all our days in his holiness, and approved in his sight.

And you, my child, will be known for a prophet of the Most High, going before the Lord, to clear his way for him.

You will make known to his people the salvation that is to release them from their sins.

Such is the merciful kindness of our God, which has bidden him come to us, like a dawning from on high.

To give light to those who live in darkness, in the shadow of death, and to guide our feet into the way of peace.

Let us pray. God who divides day from night, cause our deeds to stand out from the shades of darkness. Help us ever to set our hearts on holy things, and to live continually in your light: through our

Lord Jesus Christ, your Son, who is God, living and reigning with you, in the unity of the Holy Spirit, for ever and ever. Amen.

CANTICLE OF THE SUN

O Most High, Almighty, good Lord God, to you belong praise, glory, honor, and all blessing!

Praised be my Lord God for all his creatures, and especially for our brother the sun who brings us the day and who brings us the light; fair is he and shines with a very great splendor: O Lord, to us he signifies you!

Praised be my Lord for our sister the moon, and for the stars, which he has set clear and lovely in heaven.

Praised be my Lord for our brother the wind, and for the air and clouds, calms and all weather by which you uphold life in all creatures.

Praised be my Lord for our sister water, who is very serviceable to us and humble and precious and clean.

Praised be my Lord for our brother fire, through whom you give us light in the darkness; and he is bright and pleasant and very mighty and strong.

Praised be my Lord for our mother the earth, who sustains and keeps us, and brings forth fruits and flowers of many colors, and grass.

Praised be my Lord for all those who pardon one another for his love's sake, and who endure weakness and tribulation; blessed are they who peaceably endure, for you, O Most High, shall give them a crown.

Praised be my Lord for our sister, the death of the body, from which no one escapes.

Blessed are they who are found walking by your most holy will, for the second death shall have no power to do them harm.

Praise you and bless the Lord, and give thanks unto God, and serve God with great humility.

SAINT FRANCIS OF ASSISI

GAELIC PRAYER

Thanks to You, O God, that I have risen today.

To the rising of this life itself;

May it be to your own glory,

O God of every gift,

And to the glory of my soul likewise.

Even as I clothe my body with wool,

O God, cover my soul with the shadow of your wing.

Help me to avoid every sin,

and the source of every sin to forsake. Amen.

3. Prayers During the Day

THE ANGELUS

For centuries, the Church has recited the Angelus three times a day in honor of Christ's Incarnation and the Blessed Virgin Mary.

V. The angel of the Lord brought word to Mary;

R. and she conceived by the Holy Spirit.

Hail, Mary....

V. Behold the handmaid of the Lord;

R. let it be done to me according to your word.

Hail, Mary....

V. And the Word was made flesh;

R. and dwelt among us.

Hail, Mary....

V. Pray for us, holy Mother of God,

R. that we may be made worthy of the promises of Christ.

Let us pray.

Pour forth your grace into our hearts, we pray you, O Lord, so that we, to whom the Incarnation of Christ, your Son, was made known by the message of an angel, may by his Passion and Cross be brought to the glory of his Resurrection. We ask this through the same Christ our Lord. Amen.

REGINA CAELI

The Regina Caeli is said in place of the Angelus during Easter time.

V. Queen of heaven, rejoice! Alleluia.

R. For he whom you did merit to bear. Alleluia.

Hail, Mary....

V. Has risen, as he said. Alleluia.

R. Pray for us to God. Alleluia.

Hail, Mary....

V. Rejoice and be glad, O Virgin Mary. Alleluia.

R. For the Lord is truly risen. Alleluia.

Hail, Mary....

Let us pray.

O God, who gave joy to the world through the Resurrection of your Son our Lord Jesus Christ, grant, we beseech you, that through the intercession of the Virgin Mary, his Mother, we may obtain the joys of everlasting life, through the same Christ our Lord. Amen.

SHORT PRAYERS TO SAY THROUGHOUT THE DAY

Blessed be God. Blessed be His holy Name.

God, be merciful to me, a sinner.

O Jesus, Friend of the children, bless the children of the whole world.

Divine Heart of Jesus, convert the sinners, save the dying; deliver the holy souls in Purgatory.

Heart of Jesus, I put my trust in you.

Jesus, King and Center of all hearts, through the coming of your kingdom, give us peace.

Jesus, Mary, and Joseph, bless us now and at the hour of our death.

Come, Holy Spirit, fill the hearts of the faithful and light in them the fire of your Divine Love.

Mary, Mother of mercy, pray for us.

O Mary, bless this house where always your name is blessed.

Mary, conceived without sin, pray for us who have recourse to you.

PRAYER BEFORE THE DAY'S WORK

Direct, O Lord God, our actions this day and make them holy, guide and govern our hearts and bodies, that we may carry out our work with your grace and in accord with your law, and that every prayer and action of ours may begin always with you and through you be ended happily. Amen.

PRAYER BEFORE STUDY

Lord, my God, direct my study, ensure my perseverance, and set your seal upon its completion. You who are the fount of wisdom, shed light upon the darkness of my understanding and dispel the twofold darkness of sin and ignorance. Grant me a keen understanding, a retentive memory, method and ease in learning, fluency in speech and writing. Finally, set me on a way of life that is pleasing to you and grant me confidence that I will embrace you at the end. Amen.

SAINT THOMAS AQUINAS, ADAPTED

GRACES BEFORE MEALS

Bless us, O Lord, for these thy gifts, which we are about to receive from thy bounty, through Christ, our Lord.

R. Amen.

V. Lord, have mercy.

R. Christ, have mercy.

V. Lord, have mercy.

Our Father....(silently or aloud)

V. May the king of eternal glory make us partakers at the heavenly banquet.

R. Amen.

or

Bless us, O Lord, bless this meal and the table spread before us. Bless also those who have prepared it; and provide bread for those who have none. Amen.

or

Lord Jesus Christ, after your Resurrection you appeared to your disciples while they were at table and partook of their food. Be our invisible guest at this meal and make us feel the joy of your company. Amen.

GRACES AFTER MEALS

Father, we thank you for this food and all the daily signs of your care for this house. To you, Protector of all, be honor and glory, both now and forever. Amen.

or

We thank you, Lord, our Father in heaven. You have provided us with food, and given us the infinite riches of Christ. You comfort us in all our sorrows, that we may comfort others with the strength you give us. Thanks be to God. Amen.

SERENITY PRAYER

God grant me the serenity to accept the things I cannot change, courage to change the things I can, and the wisdom to know the difference. Living one day at a time; enjoying one moment at a time; accepting hardship as the pathway to peace. Taking as Jesus did this sinful world as it is, not as I would have it; trusting that he will make all things right if I surrender to his will; that I may be reasonably happy in this life and supremely happy with him forever in the next.

REINHOLD NIEBUHR

4. Evening Prayers

NIGHT PRAYER

Watch, dear Lord,
with those who wake, or watch, or weep tonight,
and give your angels charge over those who sleep.
Tend your sick ones, O Lord Jesus Christ,
rest your weary ones.
Bless your dying ones.
Soothe your suffering ones.
Pity your afflicted ones.
Shield your joyous ones.
And all for your love's sake,
Amen.

SAINT AUGUSTINE

PRAYER OF SAINT ALPHONSUS

Jesus Christ, my God, I adore you and thank you for all the graces you have given me this day. I offer you my sleep and all the moments of this night, and I pray that you will keep me free from sin. Therefore I place myself in your arms and under the mantle of my Mother, our Lady. Let the holy angels gather about me and keep me in peace; and let your blessing be upon me. Amen.

ANCIENT ENGLISH BEDTIME PRAYER

Matthew, Mark, Luke, and John.
Bless the bed that I lie on.
Before I lay me down to sleep
I give my soul to Christ to keep.
Four corners to my bed,
Four angels there a-spread,

Two to foot and two to head,
And four to carry me when I'm dead.
I go by sea, I go by land,
The Lord made me by his right hand.
If any danger come to me,
Sweet Jesus Christ deliver me.
He's the branch and I'm the flower,
Pray God send me a happy hour,
And if I die before I wake
I pray the Lord my soul will take.

CONFITEOR

I confess to almighty God,
to blessed Mary ever virgin,
to blessed Michael the archangel,
to blessed John the Baptist,
to the holy apostles Peter and Paul,
and to all the saints,
that I have sinned exceedingly in thought, word, and deed,
through my fault, through my fault, through my most grievous fault.
Therefore, I beseech blessed Mary ever virgin,
blessed Michael the archangel,
blessed John the Baptist,
the holy apostles Peter and Paul,
and all the saints,
to pray for me to the Lord our God. Amen.

EVENING PRAYER FROM THE LITURGY OF THE HOURS

Stay with us, Lord Jesus, for evening draws near, and be our companion on our way to set our hearts on fire with new hope. Help us to recognize your presence among us in the Scriptures that we read, and in the breaking of bread, for you live and reign with the Father and the Holy Spirit, one God forever and ever. May the Lord bless us, protect us from all evil, and bring us to everlasting life. Amen.

PRAYER FOR PEACEFUL SLEEP

Keep us, Lord, so awake in the duties of our callings that we may thus sleep in your peace and wake tomorrow in your glory.

JOHN DONNE

PRAYER AT TWILIGHT

Blessed are You, Lord our God, King of the universe.

By his word He brings on the evening twilight; in wisdom he opens the gates of dawn, and with foresight makes time pass and seasons change, according to his plan.

He creates day and night, turning light into darkness and darkness into light. He makes the day fade away and brings on the night, and separates day and night, for he is the Lord of the hosts of heaven.

Blessed are you, Lord who bring on the evening twilight. Amen.

FOR A HAPPY DEATH

Jesus, Mary, and Joseph, I give you my heart and my soul. Jesus, Mary, and Joseph, stand by me in my last agony. Jesus, Mary, and Joseph, let me draw my last breath at peace with you. Amen.

CANTICLE OF SIMEON (LUKE 2:29–32)

Now, O Lord, you can dismiss your servant in peace,
for you have fulfilled your word,
and my eyes have seen your salvation,
which you display for all the people to see.
Here is the light you will reveal to the nations and the glory of
your people Israel.

FROM THE GREEK BOOK OF HOURS

Great and most high God, who in your wisdom has built all creation, making the sun to command the day, the moon and stars to command the night, it is your grace which has brought us sinners into your presence to praise and glorify you at this evening hour. Let our prayer be wafted up to you like incense, and you, Lord, accept it as a sweet fragrance.

Grant us peace at this hour and through the coming night. Free us from nightly terrors, from all troubles that infest the darkness, and let the sleep you have given us for our repose be undisturbed by evil dreams. Thus, even as we slumber may we be mindful of you, Lord and giver of all good, and in the morning, let us rise up joyfully to glorify your goodness. Amen.

SECTION THREE

The Holy Sacrifice of the Mass

*T*he Mass, in which the bread and wine become the body and blood of our Lord Jesus Christ in memory of his sacrifice on the Cross, is the source and summit of all Catholic worship and life. It is the summit of the worship given by the faithful to the Father through Christ. Through the Mass, the mystery of redemption is represented. All other actions lead up to the sacrifice of the Eucharist or flow from it. It is at once an action of Christ himself and of his Church, the people of God. It is a banquet for Christ's family, a sign of unity and love, a gathering of God's whole people.

1. Prayers Before Mass

PRAYER OF SAINT AMBROSE

Lord, Jesus Christ, I approach your banquet table in fear and trembling, for I am a sinner, and dare not rely on my own worth but only on your goodness and mercy. I am defiled by many sins in body and soul, and by my unguarded thoughts and words.

Gracious God of majesty and awe, I seek your protection, I look for your healing. Poor troubled sinner that I am, I appeal to you, the fountain of all mercy. I cannot bear your judgment, but I trust in your salvation. Lord, I show my wounds to you and uncover my shame before you.

I know my sins are many and great, and they fill me with fear, but I hope in your mercies. Lord Jesus Christ, God and man, crucified for us, look upon me with mercy and hear my prayer.

Have mercy on me, full of sorrow and sin, for the depth of your compassion never ends. Praise to you, saving sacrifice, offered on the wood of the Cross for me and for all.

Praise to the precious blood, flowing from your wounds and washing away the sins of the whole world.

Remember, Lord, your creature, whom you have redeemed with your blood. I repent my sins, and I long to put right what I have done. Merciful Father, take away all my offenses and sins, purify me in body and soul, and make me worthy to receive your body and blood, which I intend to receive for the remission of all of my sins and the rebirth of my better instincts.

May it prompt me to do works pleasing to you and profitable to my health in body and soul, and be a firm defense against the wiles of my enemies. Amen.

PRAYER OF SAINT THOMAS AQUINAS

Almighty and eternal God, I am about to approach the sacrament of your only-begotten Son, our Lord Jesus Christ.

Sick, I draw near to the physician of life; unclean, to the fountain of mercy; blind, to the light of eternal brightness; poor and needy, to the Lord of heaven and earth. I ask you in the abundance of your goodness to heal my ills. Cleanse my sins, enlighten my blindness, enrich my poverty, and clothe my nakedness.

Make me ready to receive the Bread of angels with such reverence and humility, such sorrow and devotion, such purity and faith, such purpose and intention as shall best lead to my salvation.

Dear God, grant that I may so receive the Body of your only-begotten Son, that I may be worthy to be incorporated into his Mystical Body and counted among his members.

O most loving Father, let me see your beloved Son, whom I now intend to receive, veiled indeed in this life, revealed throughout eternity face to face. He reigns and lives with you in the unity of the Holy Spirit, God, forever and ever. Amen.

PRAYER OF INTENTION FOR THE MASS

I offer you, O God, this Mass, to the honor and glory of your holy Name, in thanksgiving for all your benefits and in satisfaction for all my sins. I offer this holy Mass in union with the offering my Redeemer made of himself upon the Cross, and in union with all the intentions my divine Savior had in the institution of the most holy sacrament. I offer this holy Mass as an atonement to the Heart of Jesus, for all the outrages it has received, from myself and from others. I also offer it for (*here name your intention*), for the conversion of sinners, the perseverance of the just, and for the relief of the souls in purgatory. Amen.

PSALM 86 (85)

Have mercy on me, O Lord, for I cry to you all day.

Bring joy to the soul of your servant, for to you, O Lord, I lift up my soul.

You are good and forgiving, O Lord, caring for those who call on you.

Listen, O Lord, to my prayer, hear the voice of my pleading.

I call on you in the time of my trouble, for you will answer me.

None is like you among the gods, your works are beyond compare.

All the nations you have made will come; they will worship before you, O Lord, and bring glory to your name.

For you are great, and wonderful are your deeds; you alone are God.

2. Order of Mass

INTRODUCTORY RITES

Entrance: We all gather together into one assembly to deepen our union among ourselves and with our Savior. We stand and sing to open the celebration.

Greeting and Veneration of the Altar: The priest, acting in the person of Christ, greets the faithful and invites the "grace of our Lord Jesus Christ and the love of God and the fellowship of the Holy Spirit" be with us always.

Penitential Rite (Confiteor): The priest invites us to search our hearts and confess our sins to God. Afterward, the priest says an absolution. Here is one of the formulas used at the Mass:

I confess to almighty God, and to you, my brothers and sisters, that I have sinned through my own fault in my thoughts and in my words, in what I have done, and in what I have failed to do; and I ask blessed Mary, ever virgin, all the angels and saints, and you, my brothers and sisters, to pray for me to the Lord our God. Amen.

Invocation to Christ (Kyrie Eleison): We acknowledge Christ as Lord and plead for his mercy. These following words are alternately prayed by the priest and the people.

Lord, have mercy.
Christ, have mercy.
Lord, have mercy.

Gloria: The Gloria is one of the most ancient morning hymns of the Church. We proclaim the praise of the Holy Trinity, joining others who have preceded us throughout the centuries. This prayer is omitted in Lent and Advent.

Glory to God in the highest,
and peace to his people on earth.
Lord God, heavenly King,
almighty God and Father,
we worship you, we give you thanks,
we praise you for your glory.
Lord Jesus Christ, only Son of the Father,
Lord God, Lamb of God,
you take away the sin of the world:
have mercy on us;
you are seated at the right hand of the Father:
receive our prayer.

For you alone are the Holy One,
you alone are the Lord,
you alone are the Most High,
   Jesus Christ,
   with the Holy Spirit,
   in the glory of God the Father. Amen.

Opening Prayer or Collect: This prayer changes with each day and expresses the theme of the eucharistic celebration. The people acclaim this prayer as their own through their concluding "Amen."

LITURGY OF THE WORD

Scripture Readings: These include the "writings of the prophets" from the Old Testament and the letters and Gospels of the New Testament.

Chants Between the Readings: The faithful adopt the Word of God as their own, and respond to it with songs from the Book of Psalms.

Homily: The Word of God enters into our own lives through the sermon which exhorts us to put the Scriptures into practice. The faithful listen with open hearts and minds to the words of the homilist.

Profession of Faith: After listening to God's word in the homily, we express our faith. We stand in order to show our readiness to make this pledge. The formula used for Sunday Masses is the Nicene Creed which follows:

We believe in one God,
   the Father, the Almighty,
   maker of heaven and earth,
   of all that is seen and unseen.

We believe in one Lord, Jesus Christ,
   the only Son of God,
   eternally begotten of the Father,
   God from God, Light from Light,
   true God from true God,
   begotten, not made, one in Being with the Father.
   Through him all things were made.
   For us men and for our salvation
      he came down from heaven:
by the power of the Holy Spirit
   he was born of the Virgin Mary,
      and became man.
For our sake he was crucified under Pontius Pilate;
   he suffered, died, and was buried.
   On the third day he rose again
      in fulfillment of the Scriptures;
   he ascended into heaven
      and is seated at the right hand of the Father.
He will come again in glory to judge the living
      and the dead,
   and his kingdom will have no end.
We believe in the Holy Spirit,
   the Lord, the giver of life,
   who proceeds from the Father and the Son.
   With the Father and the Son he is worshiped
      and glorified.
   He has spoken through the prophets.
   We believe in one holy catholic
      and apostolic Church.
   We acknowledge one baptism
   for the forgiveness of sins.

We look for the resurrection of the dead,
and the life of the world to come. Amen.

General Intercessions: Inspired by God's word, we then pray for all the needs of the Church and for the well-being of all humankind.

LITURGY OF THE EUCHARIST

Preparation of the Gifts (Offertory): Sometimes in procession, the bread and wine, the same elements that Christ used at the Last Supper, are brought to the altar and placed on it by the priest. These will be offered in sacrifice by the priest in the name of Christ, and during the offering they will become his body and blood. From the earliest days of the Church, the faithful have brought, along with the bread and wine, gifts to share with those in need. This becomes the "collection," to use for the support of the Church and the needs of those without resources.

Eucharistic Prayer: The opening part of the Eucharistic Prayer is a formal act of thanksgiving which varies according to feasts and seasons. The preface concludes with the first acclamation of the people:

Holy, holy, holy Lord, God of power and might.
Heaven and earth are full of your glory.
Hosanna in the highest!
Blessed is he who comes
in the name of the Lord.
Hosanna in the highest!

The Eucharistic Prayer is continued with one of five forms that include these four parts: the *epiclesis*, in which the Church gives thanks to the Father, through the Son and the Holy Spirit, for all of his works; the *institution narrative,* in which the Church asks the Father to send his Holy Spirit on the bread and wine, so that by his power they may become the body and blood of Jesus Christ; the *anamnesis*, in which the Church calls to mind the passion, Resurrection, and return of Jesus Christ, presenting this offering of his Son to the Father, a sacrifice which reconciles us with him; and, finally, the *intercessions,* in which the Church shows that the Eucharist is celebrated in communion with the whole Church, living and dead, in heaven and on earth.

Following Christ's command to "do this in remembrance of me," the whole congregation recalls the mystery of his death and Resurrection with one of four acclamations. The people end the Eucharistic Prayer with this final acclamation:

Through him, with him, in him,
in the unity of the Holy Spirit,
all glory and honor is yours,
almighty Father,
forever and ever.
Amen!

COMMUNION RITE

The Lord's Prayer: Since we are members of God's family, gathered around the banquet table of the Father, we can confidently call him "Our Father," as we pray the prayer he himself taught us.

Rite of Peace: Before we share the consecrated bread that will make us one, we express our love for one another and pray for peace and unity in the Church and in all of humankind. The priest says these words:

Lord Jesus Christ, you said to your apostles: I leave you peace, my peace I give you. Look not on our sins, but on the faith of your Church, and grant us the peace and unity of your kingdom, where you live and reign forever and ever.

The people respond with "Amen," and exchange the sign of peace, each with his or her neighbor.

Breaking of the Bread: Christ broke the bread to feed the crowds; he broke it at the Last Supper, and also after his Resurrection. It was in the breaking of the bread that his disciples recognized him. As the priest breaks the bread, we say or sing:

Lamb of God, you take away the sins of the world:
    have mercy on us.
Lamb of God, you take away the sins of the world:
    have mercy on us.
Lamb of God, you take away the sins of the world:
    grant us peace.

Preparation for Communion: The priest genuflects, raises the host, and facing the people says aloud:

This is the Lamb of God
who takes away the sins of the world.
Happy are those who are called to his supper.

With the people he adds:
Lord, I am not worthy to receive you,
but only say the word and I shall be healed.

Communion Procession and Song: The faithful go to Communion together in procession, responding "Amen" to the eucharistic minister's affirmation, "The Body (or Blood) of Christ."

Prayer After Communion: Priest and people pray in silence for a while, unless a period of silence has already been observed. Then the priest says or sings the Prayer after Communion, which petitions our Father that the effects of the mystery of this celebration be obtained. The faithful respond with an "Amen."

Final Blessing: The priest faces the people, extends his hands, and gives a final blessing. One formula is the one that follows:

May almighty God bless you, the Father and the Son and the Holy Spirit.

Dismissal: The dismissal rite sends us forth into the world to do good works, to praise God, and to serve our neighbor. The priest or deacon ends the Mass with one of these forms:

Go in the peace of Christ.
Go in peace to love and serve the Lord.
The Mass is ended, go in peace.

The faithful responds with:
Thanks be to God.

3. Prayers Before Communion

PRAYER OF BELIEF

This is in truth the body and blood of Emmanuel, our God. I believe, I believe, I believe, and with my last breath will proclaim that this is the living flesh which your only-begotten Son, our Lord and Savior Jesus Christ, took from our Lady Mary, the holy Mother of God, and united with his Godhead. After bearing witness to the truth before Pontius Pilate, he gave up this body, of his own free will, to die on the cross for us; gave it for our salvation, to bring forgiveness of sins and everlasting life to those who partake of it. I believe that this is the very truth. Amen.

PRAYER FROM THE BYZANTINE LITURGY

O Lord, I believe and profess that you are truly Christ, the Son of the living God, who came into the world to save sinners, of whom I am the first. Accept me as a partaker of your mystical supper, O Son of God; for I will not give you a kiss as did Judas, but like the thief I confess to you: Remember me, O Lord, when you shall come into your kingdom. Remember me, O Holy One, when you shall come into your kingdom. Amen.

PRAYER OF SAINT BONAVENTURE

My Lord, who are you, and who am I, that I should dare to take you into my body and soul? A thousand years of penance and tears would not be sufficient to make me worthy to receive so royal a sacrament even once; how much more am I unworthy of it, who fall into sin daily; I, the incorrigible, who approach you so often without due preparation. Nevertheless, your mercy infinitely surpasses my unworthiness. Therefore, I make bold to receive this sacrament, trusting in your love. Amen.

4. Prayers After Communion

PRAYER OF SUPPLICATION

Strengthened with the bread of heaven, and refreshed by a drink from the cup of eternity, let us give praise and thanksgiving to our Lord God. Let us pray that we who have received the body of our Lord Jesus Christ, may have the grace to put away the sins of the flesh and become new spiritual creatures.

Fill our hearts with joy, Lord, you who have given us the Eucharist of your sacred body, so that we who are refreshed by taking bodily food, may deserve to be filled with spiritual blessings.

Lord, grant us an unblemished life, right faith, heartfelt peace, holy patience, devout humility, and a clear conscience. May we deserve by holy living to inherit the kingdom of heaven, and there to join you in paradise, through Christ, our Lord. Amen.

PRAYER TO THE HOLY TRINITY

We thank you, almighty Father, who has prepared a holy Church to be a place of rest for us and a haven of holiness where the Holy Trinity is glorified. Alleluia.

We thank you, Christ, who has bestowed on us life by your life-giving body and holy blood. Grant us forgiveness and your great mercy. Alleluia.

We thank you, Spirit of truth, who has renewed your holy Church. Keep her faith in the Trinity unshaken henceforth and forever. Amen.

PRAYER TO THE HOLY MOTHER OF GOD

Dearest Virgin Mother, who was deemed worthy to conceive by the Holy Spirit and to bear in your womb the same Lord whom I have just received, plead for me and obtain his forgiveness of any failing or lack of reverence of which I have been guilty while receiving this most holy sacrament. Amen.

PRAYER OF THE CURÉ OF ARS

My Jesus, from eternity it has been your plan to give yourself to us in the sacrament of your love. Therefore, you have implanted in us such longing as you alone can satisfy.

I may go from here to the other end of the world, from riches to greater riches, from pleasure to pleasure, and still I shall not be content. All the world cannot satisfy the immortal soul.

Sweet it is when we set our hearts on loving you, my God. It sometimes happens that the more we know our neighbors, the less we love them; but with you, O God, it is never so. The more we know, the more we love you.

My Jesus, how sweet it is to love you. Let me be like the disciples on Mount Tabor, seeing nothing else but you, my Savior. Let us be as two friends, neither of whom can ever offend the other. Amen.

PRAYER OF SAINT THOMAS AQUINAS

Lord, Father, all-powerful and ever-living God,
I thank you, for even though I am a sinner,
your unprofitable and unworthy servant,
in the kindness of your mercy,
you have fed me with the precious body and blood of your Son,
our Lord Jesus Christ.
I pray that this holy Communion
may bring me not condemnation and punishment,
but forgiveness and salvation.
May it be a helmet of faith
and a shield of good will.
May it purify me from evil ways
and put an end to my wayward passions.
May it bring me charity and patience,
humility and obedience,
and growth in the power to do good.
May it be my strong defense
against all my enemies, visible and invisible,
and the perfect calming of all my evil impulses,
bodily and spiritual.
May it unite me more closely to you,
   the one true God,
and lead me safely through death
to everlasting happiness with you.
And I pray that you will lead me, a sinner,
to the banquet where you,

with your Son and Holy Spirit,
are true and perfect light,
total fulfillment, everlasting joy,
gladness without end,
and perfect happiness to your saints.
Grant this through Christ our Lord. Amen.

PRAYER OF PADRE PIO AFTER HOLY COMMUNION

Stay with me, Lord, for it is necessary to have you present so that I do not forget you. You know how easily I abandon you.

Stay with me, Lord, because I am weak and I need your strength, that I may not fall so often.

Stay with me, Lord, for you are my light and without you I am in darkness.

Stay with me, Lord, to show me your will.

Stay with me, Lord, so that I hear your voice and follow you.

Stay with me, Lord, for I desire to love you very much and always be in your company.

Stay with me, Lord, if you wish me to be faithful to you.

Stay with me, Lord, as poor as my soul is I want it to be a place of consolation for you, a nest of love.

Stay with me Jesus, for it is getting late and the day is coming to a close and as life passes, death, judgment, and eternity approach. It is necessary to renew my strength, so that I will not stop along the way and for that, I need you. It is getting late and death approaches, I fear the darkness, the temptations, the dryness, the cross, the sorrows. How I need you, my Jesus, in this night of exile!

Let me recognize you as your disciples did at the breaking of the bread, so that the eucharistic Communion be the light which disperses the darkness, the force which sustains me, the unique joy of my heart.

Stay with me, Lord, because at the hour of my death, I want to remain united to you, if not by Communion, at least by grace and love.

Stay with me, Lord, for it is you alone I look for, your love, your grace, your will, your heart, your spirit, because I love you and ask no other reward but to love you more and more.

With a firm love, I will love you with all my heart while on earth and continue to love you perfectly during all eternity. Amen.

5. Prayers After Mass

PRAYER TO OUR REDEEMER

Soul of Christ, sanctify me.
Body of Christ, heal me.
Blood of Christ, cover me.
Water from the side of Christ, wash me.
Passion of Christ, strengthen me.
Good Jesus, hear me.
In your wounds shelter me.
From turning away keep me.
From the evil one protect me.
At the hour of my death call me.
Into your presence lead me,
to praise you with all your saints
forever and ever. Amen.

THE UNIVERSAL PRAYER

Lord, I believe in you; increase my faith.
I trust in you; strengthen my trust.
I love you: let me love you more and more.
I am sorry for my sins: deepen my sorrow.
I worship you as my first beginning,
I long for you as my last end,

I praise you as my constant helper,
and call on you as my loving protector.
Guide me by your wisdom,
correct me with your justice,
comfort me with your mercy,
protect me with your power.
I offer you, Lord, my thoughts: to be fixed on you;
my words: to have you for their theme;
my actions: to reflect my love for you;
my sufferings: to be endured for your greater glory.
I want to do what you ask of me:
in the way you ask,
for as long as you ask,
because you ask it.
Lord, enlighten my understanding,
strengthen my will,
purify my heart,
and make me holy.
Help me to repent of my past sins
and to rise above my human weakness
and to grow stronger as a Christian.
Let me love you, my Lord and my God,
and see myself as I really am:
a pilgrim in this world,
a Christian called to respect and love
all whose lives I touch,
those in authority over me
or those under my authority,
my friends and my enemies.
Help me to conquer anger by gentleness,
greed by generosity, apathy by fervor.
Help me to forget myself

and reach out toward others.
Make me prudent in planning,
courageous in taking risks.
Make me patient in suffering,
unassuming in prosperity.
Keep me, Lord, attentive in prayer,
temperate in food and drink,
diligent in my work,
firm in my good intentions.
Let my conscience be clear,
my conduct without fault,
my speech blameless,
my life well-ordered.
Put me on guard against my human weaknesses.
Let me cherish your love for me,
keep your law,
and come at last to your salvation.
Teach me to realize that this world is passing,
that my true future is the happiness of heaven,
that life on earth is short,
and the life to come eternal.
Help me to prepare for death
with a proper fear of judgment,
but a greater trust in your goodness.
Lead me safely through death
   to the endless joy of heaven.
Grant this through Christ our Lord. Amen.

ATTRIBUTED TO POPE CLEMENT XI

CANTICLE OF THE THREE CHILDREN

Let us sing the hymn of the three children, which these holy ones
sang of old in the fiery furnace, giving praise to the Lord.

Bless the Lord, all you works of the Lord;
praise and exalt him above all forever.
Heavens, bless the Lord;
angels of the Lord, bless the Lord.
Sun and moon, bless the Lord;
stars of heaven, bless the Lord.
Every shower and dew, bless the Lord;
all you winds, bless the Lord.
Fire and heat, bless the Lord;
cold and heat, bless the Lord.
Dews and hoar frosts, bless the Lord;
frost and cold, bless the Lord;
ice and snow, bless the Lord;
nights and days, bless the Lord.
Light and darkness, bless the Lord;
lightning and clouds, bless the Lord.
Let the earth bless the Lord;
let it praise and exalt him above all forever.
Mountains and hills, bless the Lord;
everything growing from the earth, bless the Lord.
Seas and rivers, bless the Lord;
fountains, bless the Lord.
Whales and all that move in the waters,
     bless the Lord;
all you fowls of the air, bless the Lord.
All you beasts and cattle, bless the Lord;
sons of men, bless the Lord.
Israel, bless the Lord;
praise and exalt him above all forever.
Priests of the Lord, bless the Lord;
servants of the Lord, bless the Lord.
Spirits and souls of the just, bless the Lord;

holy men of humble heart, bless the Lord.
Ananias, Azarias, and Misael, bless the Lord;
praise and exalt him above all forever.
Let us bless the Father and the Son,
    with the Holy Spirit;
let us praise and exalt him above all forever.
Blessed are you, Lord, in the firmament of heaven;
and worthy of praise, and glorious
    above all forever.

THANKSGIVING OF BALDWIN OF CANTERBURY

How great is your goodness, Lord, who does not shrink from letting your servant place you upon his heart! How great my own worth, since you have chosen me to have part in yours, to have you abiding in me, to love you as you deserve, above myself.

Lord, take from me this hard heart, and give me a new, clean heart of flesh and blood. You who make my heart pure, take possession of mine and make it your home. Hold it and fill it, you who are higher than my topmost height, more inward than my inward being. You, the seal of holiness, beauty of all beauties, engrave on my heart your image and the imprint of your mercy. Be, O God, my eternal love and my inheritance. Amen.

Sacrament of Penance and Reconciliation

*T*he Second Vatican Council says, in <u>Lumen Gentium</u>, that "those who approach the sacrament of Penance obtain pardon from God's mercy for the offense committed against him and are, at the same time, reconciled with the Church which they have wounded by their sins" (§2). Thus the faithful who fall into sin after baptism can be reconciled with God and renewed in grace.

Sin, first of all, is an offense against God, and thus the most essential purpose of the sacrament of penance is to reconcile sinners with the Father, who first loved them, with Christ, who gave himself on the Cross for them, and with the Holy Spirit who has been poured out on them in abundance.

Secondly, the Church is made up of sinners who individually and as a group fall short of the gospel ideals. Such common and sometimes public sins require confession, repentance, and penance.

A sinner must approach the sacrament of penance with the appropriate disposition. This entails four actions: (1) Conversion: a sincere repentance, a heartfelt sorrow, and an intent to sin no more; (2) Confession: disclosure of one's sins before a priest; (3) Acts of penance: performance of certain acts in order to repair the harm caused by the sin and provide a cure for the sickness of sin; and, (4) Absolution: pardon pronounced by the priest in the name of Christ who has given him this power (CCC §1420– 1498).

1. Prayers Before Confession

PRAYER OF SAINT JOHN OF THE CROSS

Lord God, my Beloved, if you are still mindful of my sins and will not grant my petitions, let your will be done, for that is my chief desire. Show your goodness and mercy, and you shall be known for them. If you are waiting for me to do good works, and upon their performance you will grant my petitions, cause them to be accomplished in me. Send also the punishment for my sins that is acceptable to you. For how will I raise myself up to you, born and bred as I am in misery, unless you, Lord, will lift me up with the hand that made me? Amen.

PRAYER FOR RECONCILIATION

Holy Lord, almighty Father, look upon me, your servant, who is overwhelmed by the storms of this world and in tears pleads guilty to all manner of transgressions. Have pity on my sighs and tears, and call me back from darkness into light. Heal me when I confess, save me when I do penance, and help my wounds to become whole. Let the enemy have no more power over my spirit. Graciously receive my confession, purify me, and bring me back to your grace, through this reconciling sacrament through which I give thanks to your holy Name. Amen.

PRAYER OF SAINT CATHERINE OF SIENA

Merciful Lord, it does not surprise me that you forget completely the sins of those who repent. I am not surprised that you remain faithful to those who revile you. The mercy which pours forth from you fills the whole world. It was by your mercy that we were created, and by your mercy that you redeemed us by sending your Son. Your mercy is the light in which sinners find you, and good people come back to you. Your mercy is everywhere. Your justice is constantly tempered with mercy, so you refuse to punish us as we deserve. O my Lover! It was not enough that you took on our humanity; you had to die for us as well. Amen.

PRAYER OF WILLIAM OF SAINT THIERRY

Pardon us, O Lord, pardon us. We beg to shift the blame for our sins; we make excuses. But no one can hide from the light of your truth, which both enlightens those who turn to it, and exposes those who turn away. Even our blood and our bones are visible to you, who created us out of dust. How foolish we are to think that we can rule our own lives, satisfying our own desires, without thought of you. How stupid we are to imagine that we can keep our sins hidden. But although we may deceive other people, we cannot deceive you. And since you see into our hearts, we cannot deceive ourselves, for your light reveals to us our own spiritual corruption. Let us, therefore, fall down before you, weeping with tears of shame. May your judgment give new shape to our souls. May your power mold our hearts to reflect your love. May your grace infuse our minds, so that our thoughts reflect your will. Amen.

EXAMINATION OF CONSCIENCE

In an examination of conscience, before the sacrament of penance, each person should ask these questions in particular:

1. What is my attitude to the sacrament of penance? Do I sincerely want to be set free from sin, to turn again to God, to begin a new life, and to enter into a deeper friendship with God? Or do I look on it as a burden, to be undertaken as seldom as possible?
2. Did I forget to mention, or deliberately conceal, any grave sins in past confessions?
3. Did I perform the penance I was given? Did I make reparation for any injury to others? Have I tried to put into practice my resolution to lead a better life in keeping with the gospel?

Each person should next examine his or her life in the light of God's word, personalizing these questions and using them as guidelines:

The Lord says: "You shall love the Lord your God with your whole heart."

1. Is my heart set on God, so that I really love him above all things

and am faithful to his commandments, as children love their fathers? Or am I more concerned about the things of the world? Have I a right intention in what I do?

2. God spoke to us in his Son. Is my faith in God firm and secure? Am I wholehearted in accepting the Church's teaching? Have I been careful to grow in my understanding of the faith, to hear God's word, to listen to instructions on the faith, to avoid dangers to faith? Have I been always strong and fearless in professing my faith in God and the Church? Have I been willing to be known as a Christian in private and public life?

3. Have I prayed morning and evening? When I pray, do I really raise my mind and heart to God, or is it a matter of words only? Do I offer God my difficulties, my joys, and my sorrows? Do I turn to God in time of temptation?

4. Have I love and reverence for God's name? Have I offended him in blasphemy, swearing falsely, or taking his name in vain? Have I shown disrespect for the Blessed Virgin Mary and the saints?

5. Do I keep Sundays and feast days holy by taking a full part, with attention and devotion, in the liturgy, and especially in the Mass? Have I fulfilled the precept of annual confession and of Communion during the Easter season?

6. Are there false gods that I worship by giving them greater attention and deeper trust than I give to God (for example, money, superstition, spiritism, or other occult practices)?

The Lord says: "Love one another as I have loved you."

1. Have I a genuine love for my neighbors? Or do I use them for my own ends, or do to them what I would not want done to myself? Have I given grave scandal by my words or actions?

2. In my family life, have I contributed to the well-being and happiness of the rest of the family by patience and genuine love?

Have I been obedient to parents, showing them proper respect and giving them help in their spiritual and material needs?

3. Do I share my possessions with the less fortunate? Do I do my best to help the victims of oppression, misfortune, and poverty? Or do I look down on my neighbor, especially the poor, the sick, the elderly, strangers, and people of other races?

4. Does my life reflect the mission I received in confirmation? Do I share in the apostolic and charitable works of the Church and in the life of my parish community? Have I helped to meet the needs of the Church and of the world and prayed for them: for unity in the Church, for the spread of the gospel among the nations, for peace and justice, and so on?

5. Am I concerned for the good and prosperity of the human community in which I live, or do I spend my life caring only for myself? Do I share to the best of my ability in the work of promoting justice, morality, harmony, and love in human relations? Have I done my duty as a citizen?

6. In my work or profession, am I just, hard-working, honest, serving society out of love for others? Have I been faithful to my promises and contracts?

7. Have I obeyed legitimate authority and given it due respect?

8. If I am in a position of responsibility or authority, do I use this for my advantage or for the good of others, in a spirit of service?

9. Have I been truthful and fair, or have I injured others by deceit, calumny, detraction, rash judgment, or violation of a secret?

10. Have I done violence to others by damage to life or limb, reputation, honor, or material possessions? Have I involved them in loss? Have I been responsible for advising an abortion or procuring one? Have I kept up hatred for others? Am I estranged from others through quarrels, enmity, insults, anger? Have I been guilty of refusing to testify to the innocence of another because of selfishness?

11. Have I stolen the property of others? Have I desired it unjustly and inordinately? Have I damaged it? Have I made restitution of other people's property and made good on their loss?

12. If I have been injured, have I been ready to make peace for the love of Christ and to forgive, or do I harbor hatred and the desire for revenge?

Christ our Lord says: "Be perfect as your Father is perfect."

1. Where is my life really leading me? Is the hope of eternal life my inspiration? Have I tried to grow in the life of the Spirit through prayer, reading the Word of God and mediating on it, receiving the sacraments, self-denial? Have I been anxious to control my vices, my bad inclinations and passions (for example, envy, love of food and drink)? Have I been proud and boastful, thinking myself better in the sight of God and despising others as less important than myself? Have I imposed my own will on others, without respecting their freedom and rights?

2. What use have I made of time, of health and strength, or the gifts God has given me to be used like the talents in the gospel? Did I use them to become more perfect every day? Or have I been lazy and too much given to leisure?

3. Have I been patient in accepting the sorrows and disappointments of life? How have I performed mortification so as to "fill up what is wanting to the sufferings of Christ"? Have I kept the precept of fasting and abstinence?

4. Have I kept my senses and my whole body pure and chaste as a temple of the Holy Spirit, consecrated for resurrection and glory and as a sign of God's faithful love for men and women, a sign that is seen most perfectly in the sacrament of matrimony? Have I dishonored my body by fornication, impurity, unworthy conversation and thoughts, evil desires, or

temptations? Have I given in to sensuality? Have I indulged in reading, conversation, shows, and entertainment that offend against Christian and human decency? Have I encouraged others to sin by my own failure to maintain these standards?

5. Have I gone against my conscience out of fear or hypocrisy?
6. Have I always tried to act in the true freedom of the sons and daughters of God according to the law of the Spirit, or am I the slave of forces within me?

FROM *THE RITES OF THE CATHOLIC CHURCH, VOL. 1*

2. Order of Individual Confession

WELCOME OF THE PENITENT

The penitent makes the Sign of the Cross and is invited by the priest to have trust in God with words such as the following:

May the Lord Jesus Christ welcome you. He came to call sinners, not the just. Have confidence in him.

PROCLAMATION OF THE WORD OF GOD

Either the priest or the penitent may read or say by heart some words from Scripture about repentance and the mercy of God, for example:

"Lord, you know all things; you know that I love you" (Jn 21:17).

CONFESSION OF SINS

The penitent confesses his sins. The priest may help in this and at the end give relevant advice, imposes the penance, and invites the penitent to show sorrow for sins.

PRAYER OF THE PENITENT

The penitent expresses sorrow for his or her sin. This may be done by reciting any of the following suitable prayers:

Jesus, Son of God, have mercy on me, a sinner.

Father, I have sinned against you and am not worthy to be called your son. Be merciful to me, a sinner.

My God, I am sorry for my sins with all my heart. In choosing to do wrong and failing to do good, I have sinned against you, whom I should love above all things. I firmly intend, with your help, to do penance, to sin no more, and to avoid whatever leads me to sin. Our Lord Jesus Christ suffered and died for us. In his name, my God, have mercy.

IMPOSITION OF HANDS AND ABSOLUTION

The priest extends his hands over the penitent's head and says the following:

God, the Father of mercies, through the death and Resurrection of his Son, has reconciled the world to himself and sent the Holy Spirit among us for the forgiveness of sins; through the ministry of the Church, may God give you pardon and peace, and I absolve you from your sins in the name of the Father, and of the Son, and of the Holy Spirit.

DISMISSAL

The priest dismisses the penitent who has been reconciled, using any of the acceptable forms, such as the following:

The Lord has freed you from your sins. Go in peace.

3. Prayers After Confession

PRAYER OF RESOLUTION

O my God: Henceforth I resolve to strive earnestly to be patient and gentle, and not to allow the waters of contradiction to extinguish the fire of that charity which I owe to my neighbor.

PRAYER OF SAINT FRANCIS DE SALES

Do not look forward to the changes and chances of this life with fear. Rather, look to them with full confidence that, as they arise, God to whom you belong will in his love enable you to profit by them. He has guided you thus far in life. Do you but hold fast to his dear hand, and he will lead you safely through all trials. Whenever you cannot stand, he will carry you lovingly in his arms.

Do not look forward to what may happen tomorrow. The same Eternal Father who takes care of you today will take care of you tomorrow, and every day of your life. Either he will shield you from suffering or he will give you unfailing strength to bear it.

Be at peace then, and put aside all useless thoughts, all vain dreads and all anxious imaginations.

PRAYER FOR HELP

Great God, arise; come to my rescue. For my sake rescue me from myself. You will save me from myself by defending me against the enemies within, enemies born with me and in me, who conspire to deflect me from the good resolution I have made; but you will also save me for myself, since it will be for the good of my soul and the advancement of my salvation.

PRAYER FOR LASTING REPENTANCE

I give you thanks, Lord, because you have not dealt with me as my sins deserved, but have judged me with surpassing mercy and cast all my sins into the depths of the sea.

I would gladly melt into tears, until my sins were washed away and you would smile on me again! But my soul has become a waterless desert, my strength has dried up like clay in a kiln.

Look upon me and pity me, and make the waters of contrition flow to cleanse and heal my soul. Confirm the grace you have wrought in me; accept and welcome my confession and make good on all its defects.

Let me no more go astray after the empty joys of this life; for day follows day and year succeeds year, and behold, I make no progress. Turn your face toward me and be ever ready to hear the prayer of your unworthy servant. Do not regard my sins even if my offenses have earned damnation. You have the power to save me and receive me back again into your favor, my God and my Help!

PENITENTIAL PSALM 6

O Lord, in your anger do not reprove; nor punish me in your fury.

Have mercy on me, O Lord, for I have no strength left. O Lord, heal me, for my bones are in torment.

My soul also is greatly troubled. How long, O Lord, how long? How long will you be?

Come back to me, O Lord, save my life; rescue me for the sake of your love.

For no one remembers you in the grave; who will praise you in the world of the dead?

I am weary with moaning; I weep every night, drenching my bed with tears.

My eyes have grown dim from troubles; I have weakened because of my foes.

Away from me, you evildoers, for the Lord has heard my plaintive voice.

The Lord has heard my plea; the Lord will grant all that I pray for.

Let my enemies fall back in shame, all of a sudden—the whole bunch of them!

PENITENTIAL PSALM 130 (129)

Out of the depths I cry to you, O Lord,
O Lord, hear my voice! Let your ears pay attention
    to the voice of my supplication.
If you should mark our evil, O Lord, who could stand?
But with you is forgiveness, and for that you are revered.
I waited for the Lord, my soul waits,
    and I put my hope in his word.
My soul expected the Lord more than watchmen the dawn.
O Israel, hope in the Lord, for with him is unfailing love
    and with him full deliverance.
He will deliver Israel from all its sins.

SECTION FIVE

Prayers to Jesus Christ

1. Prayers to Christ Crucified

STATIONS OF THE CROSS (WAY OF THE CROSS)

This devotion arose in Jerusalem during the Middle Ages when pilgrims retraced the steps of the "Via Dolorosa," the distance from the Praetorium, where Jesus was condemned, to Calvary, where he was crucified. For this purpose, one visits a certain number of stations (fourteen since the sixteenth century), stopping before each and meditating on the passion of Christ. All that is required in this devotional practice is to meditate on Christ's passion; what each station is about does not really matter. Thus, new Stations of the Cross which stress Scripture or different aspects of the passion have been developed. The following meditation and prayers follow the traditional stations.

Prayer of Preparation. Most merciful Jesus! With a penitent spirit I now perform this devotion in honor of your passion and death. I adore you as my God and thank you for the love with which you did make the painful journey to Calvary and did die upon the Cross for my salvation. I am truly sorry for all my sins, because by them I have offended you, and promise to amend my life. Grant that I may gain all the indulgences which are attached to this devotion. Since you have promised to draw all things to your heart, draw my love to you, that I may live and die in union with you. Amen.

Station 1: Jesus Is Condemned to Death. We adore you, O Christ, and praise you, because by your Cross you have redeemed the world.

The holy and innocent Jesus was judged by sinners and put to death. Yet, while they judged him, they were compelled to acquit him. Judas, who betrayed him, said, "I have sinned in that I have betrayed the innocent." Pilate, who sentenced him, said: "I am innocent of the blood of this just person," and placed the guilt upon the Jews. The centurion who saw him crucified said, "Indeed this was a just man."

Thus, O Lord, you are ever justified in your words, and do overcome when you are judged. And so, at the last day, when they say "They shall look on him whom they pierced"; and he who was condemned shall judge the world in power, and even those who are condemned will confess that his judgment is just.

Our Father….; Hail Mary….

Lord Jesus, crucified, have mercy on us.

Station 2: Jesus Receives and Carries His Cross. We adore you, O Christ, and praise you, because by your Cross you have redeemed the world.

Jesus supports the whole world by his divine power, for he is God; but the weight was less heavy than was the Cross which our sins had made for him. Our sins cost him this humiliation. He had to take on our human nature and appear among us as a man to offer up for us the greatest sacrifice. He had to endure a life of suffering and his passion and death at the end of it.

O Lord God almighty, who bears the weight of the whole world, who bears the weight of all our sins, preserve our bodies by your providence and be the savior of our souls by your precious blood.

O my Jesus, let me joyfully embrace your Cross and accept my own sufferings which pale beside yours.

Our Father….; Hail Mary….

Lord Jesus, crucified, have mercy on us.

Station 3: Jesus Falls Under the Weight of the Cross for the First Time. We adore you, O Christ, and praise you, because by your holy Cross you have redeemed the world.

Satan fell from heaven in the beginning; and by the just sentence of his Creator he fell, against whom he had rebelled. And when Satan had succeeded in gaining humankind to join him in his rebellion, and his Maker came to effect salvation for the fallen, then his hour of triumph came, and he made the most of it.

When Jesus had taken flesh and was in Satan's power, he determined to strike down the Holy One as he himself had been felled by the Almighty. Thus, it was that Jesus fell down so heavily onto the ground.

Dear Lord, by this your first fall, raise us all out of sin who have so miserably fallen under its power. Help me to take up my own cross and follow you.

Our Father....; Hail Mary....

Lord Jesus, crucified, have mercy on us.

Station 4: Jesus Meets His Mother. We adore you, O Christ, and praise you, because by your holy Cross you have redeemed the world.

No part of the history of salvation excludes Mary. There are those servants of Jesus who think that her work was ended when she bore him, and after that she had nothing to do but disappear and be forgotten. But we, O Lord, your children, do not think so of your Mother. She brought the infant into the temple, she lifted him up in her arms when the Magi came to adore him. She fled with him to Egypt, she took him up to Jerusalem when he was twelve years old. He lived with her at Nazareth for thirty years. She was with him at the marriage feast of Cana. And now she shows herself as he bears the sacred Cross on his shoulders.

Sweet Mother, let us ever think of you when we think of Jesus, and when we pray to him, aid us by your powerful intercession. Mother of sorrows, let me carry some of your sorrow so that I may enjoy your assistance in the hour of my death.

Our Father....; Hail Mary....

Lord Jesus, crucified, have mercy on us.

Station 5: Simon of Cyrene Helps Jesus to Carry the Cross. We adore you, O Christ, and praise you, because by your holy Cross you have redeemed the world.

Jesus permits Simon of Cyrene to assist him in carrying his Cross in order to remind us that we must take part in his suffering. He calls and we must carry on his work. His merit is infinite, yet he allows us to add our small measure of merit to it. The holiness of the Blessed Virgin, the blood of the martyrs, the sufferings of the saints, the good works of the faithful take part in that work which is perfect without them. He saves us by his blood sacrifice, but it is through and with our own that he saves us.

Dear Lord, let me follow in your footsteps, answer your invitation, and sanctify all my sufferings so that I may be with you in eternity.

Our Father....; Hail Mary....

Lord Jesus, crucified, have mercy on us.

Station 6: Veronica Wipes the Face of Jesus. We adore you, O Christ, and praise you, because by your holy Cross you have redeemed the world.

Veronica wipes the face of Jesus with her veil, and Jesus imprints on it his face. He did this to remind us all that his image must ever be impressed on all our hearts. Whoever we are, in whatever part of the earth, Jesus must live in our hearts. We may differ from each other in many things, but in this goal we must all agree. We must ever meditate on Christ's death and Resurrection and always imitate his divine excellence.

Lord, let our faces be ever pleasing in your sight, not disfigured with sin, but washed pure with your precious blood.

Our Father....; Hail Mary....

Lord Jesus, crucified, have mercy on us.

Station 7: Jesus Falls the Second Time. We adore you, O Christ, and praise you, because by your holy Cross you have redeemed the world.

Satan had a second fall when he tempted our Lord in the desert, daring to take up the Savior in his arms, showing him all kingdoms, and promising to give them to him, if only his Maker will adore him. Jesus answered, "Begone, Satan," and Satan fell down from the high mountain. And Jesus bore witness to it when he said, "I saw Satan, as lightning, falling from heaven." Satan remembered this second defeat, and now he struck down the innocent Lord a second time, now that the Evil One had him in his power.

Dear Lord, teach us to suffer with you, and not be afraid of Satan and instead rely on the strength of your grace without which we can do nothing.

Our Father....; Hail Mary....

Lord Jesus, crucified, have mercy on us.

Station 8: The Women of Jerusalem Mourn for Our Lord. We adore you, O Christ, and praise you, because by your holy Cross you have redeemed the world.

The devoted women of Jerusalem weep over the suffering of the Savior. Yet, he says to them: "The days are coming when people will say, 'Blessed are the barren, and the wombs that have not borne, and the breasts which have not given suck.'"

Lord, we do not know what is good for us, and what is bad. We cannot foretell the future, nor do we know, when you come to visit us, in what form you will come. Let us ever gaze on you, and do you look on us, and give us the grace of your bitter Cross and passion, and console us in your own way and at your own time.

Our Father....; Hail Mary....

Lord Jesus, crucified, have mercy on us.

Station 9: Jesus Falls the Third Time. We adore you, O Christ, and praise you, because by your holy Cross you have redeemed the world.

Satan will have a third and final fall at the end of the world. He knew this was to be his end; but in his despair, he knew that no suffering which he could inflict on the Savior could save him from that inevitable fiery imprisonment. Therefore, in a terrible rage, he fiercely struck down the great King for the third time.

O Jesus, only-begotten Son of God, we give you thanks that you, who are the Word Incarnate, should have permitted yourself to be humiliated once more. Let this fall enkindle in me an earnest desire to never again relapse into sin.

Our Father....; Hail Mary....

Lord Jesus, crucified, have mercy on us.

Station 10: Jesus Is Stripped of His Garments. We adore you, O Christ, and praise you, because by your holy Cross you have redeemed the world.

Jesus gave up everything of this world before he left it. He exercised the most perfect poverty. Even when he left Nazareth, and went out to preach, he had not a place to lay his head. He lived on what was given to him by those who loved him. And, therefore, he chose a death in which not even his clothes were left to him. He parted with what has seemed most necessary since the fall of human nature in the Garden of Eden.

Grant us in a similar manner, O Lord, to care nothing for anything on earth, and to bear the loss of all things, and to endure even shame, contempt, and mockery rather than have you be ashamed of us on the last day.

Our Father....; Hail Mary....

Lord Jesus, crucified, have mercy on us.

Station 11: Jesus Is Nailed to the Cross. We adore you, O Christ, and praise you, because by your holy Cross you have redeemed the world.

Jesus is pierced through each hand and foot with nails. His eyes are dimmed with blood and are closed with swollen lids which the blows of his executioners have caused. His mouth is filled with vinegar and gall. His head is encircled by the sharp thorns. His heart is pierced with the spear. Thus, all his senses are mortified and crucified, that he may make atonement for every kind of human sin.

O Jesus, crucify us with you. Let us never sin by hand or foot, by eyes or mouth, or by head or heart. Let all our senses be a sacrifice to you; let every part of our bodies sing your praise. Let the sacred blood which flowed from your five wounds anoint us with such grace that we may die to the world, and live only for you.

Our Father....; Hail Mary....

Lord Jesus, crucified, have mercy on us.

Station 12: Jesus Dies Upon the Cross. We adore you, O Christ, and praise you, because by your holy Cross you have redeemed the world.

The earthly life of Jesus has come to an end, and the mystery of God's love toward us is accomplished. The price is paid, and we are redeemed. The eternal Father determined not to pardon us without a price. He might have saved us with a mere act of his will. But to show his love for us he set a price to be taken for the guilt of our sins, and this price was nothing less than the death of his Son.

O my God and Father, you have valued us so much you were willing to pay the highest of all possible prices for our sinful souls. Should we not love and choose you above all things as the one necessary and only good?

Our Father....; Hail Mary....

Lord Jesus, crucified, have mercy on us.

Station 13: Jesus Is Taken Down From the Cross and Laid in the Arms of His Blessed Mother. We adore you, O Christ, and praise you, because by your holy Cross you have redeemed the world.

He is once again in your arms, O Virgin Mother. He went out from you to do his Father's work—and he has done it and suffered. He has not been in your arms, O Mother of God, since he was a child, but now you have a claim on him, when the world has done its worst. We can only rejoice in this great mystery. Now that he is placed on your lap, O sinless Mother, may we also persevere to the end and receive the body and blood of Christ in the sacrament of the Eucharist with a pure heart.

Our Father....; Hail Mary....

Lord Jesus, crucified, have mercy on us.

Station 14: Jesus Is Laid in the Sepulcher. We adore you, O Christ, and praise you, because by your holy Cross you have redeemed the world.

Jesus, when he was nearest to his everlasting triumph, seemed to be farthest from it. He was lying dead in a cave, wrapped in burying clothes, and confined within a tomb of stone. Soon he would have a glorified body and would ascend on high.

O Jesus, let us trust in you, so that the greater our distress, the nearer we are to you. The more we are scorned, the more you will honor us and the higher you will exalt us. The more we are forgotten, the more you will keep us in mind. The more we are abandoned, the closer you will bring us to your heart.

Our Father....; Hail Mary....

Lord Jesus, crucified; have mercy on us.

Concluding Prayer. Almighty God, merciful Father, who has given us your beloved Son as an example of humility, obedience, and patience as a means to show us the Way of Life, bearing the Cross: grant that we may take on the sweet yoke of his gospel, following him as true disciples so that we may one day rise with him in glory, world without end. Amen.

DEVOTION TO THE SEVEN WORDS SPOKEN FROM THE CROSS

First Word: Father, Forgive Them, For They Know Not What They Do. O Jesus, who hung in agony upon the Cross out of love for me, and by your pains paid for my sins, you who spoke of pardon for your persecutors, obtain pardon for all those who are now facing death, and have pity on me when I am facing mine. By the merits of your precious blood shed for our salvation, grant us continual sorrow for our sins so that we may share eternal life with you. Amen.

Have mercy on us, O Lord.

My God, I believe in you, I hope in you, I love you. I am sorry for my sins because by them I have offended you.

Second Word: This Day Shall You Be With Me In Paradise. My Jesus, who in agony on the Cross, did readily respond to the faith of the good thief who acknowledged you as the Son of God, you who assured him of a place in heaven, pity all of those who are facing death and pity me when I am facing mine. By the merit of your precious blood, shed for us, wake up in our souls a firm and steadfast faith. Protect us from the temptations of Satan so that we may obtain the prize of holy paradise with you forever. Amen.

Have mercy on us, O Lord.

My God, I believe in you, I hope in you, I love you. I am sorry for my sins because by them I have offended you.

The Third Word: Behold Your Son; Behold Your Mother. Oh Jesus, who out of love for me hung in agony on the Cross and who left your own most holy Mother as a sign of your love so that through her intercession we might seek your assistance, have pity on us. Have pity on all the faithful who are facing death and have pity on me when I also shall face mine. By the sorrows of your dear Mother, nurture in our hearts a hope that, through the merits of your precious blood, we may escape the sentence of eternal death in hell. Amen.

Have mercy on us, O Lord.

My God, I believe in you, I hope in you, I love you. I am sorry for my sins because by them I have offended you.

The Fourth Word: My God! My God! Why Have You Forsaken Me? O Jesus, out of love for me you hung in agony upon the Cross. While bodily suffering and indignities were heaped upon you, the most desperate desolation of spirit was being forsaken by your eternal Father. Have pity on all the faithful who are facing death, and pity me when I too shall be facing mine. By the merits of your precious blood, may we patiently suffer our last agony, and may we join our pains with yours so that we may be made partakers of your glory in paradise. Amen.

Have mercy on us, O Lord.

My God, I believe in you, I hope in you, I love you. I am sorry for my sins because by them I have offended you.

The Fifth Word: I Thirst. O Jesus, in agony you hung upon the Cross for me. You suffered unquenchable physical thirst and an insatiable tolerance for insults and sufferings. Yet the more you suffered so that all people might be saved, the more you demonstrated the enormous love you had in your heart. Pity all the faithful who are now facing death, and pity me when I also shall be facing mine. By the merits of your precious blood, fire in our hearts such a great love that we will be made one with you for all eternity. Amen.

Have mercy on us, O Lord.

My God, I believe in you, I hope in you, I love you. I am sorry for my sins because by them I have offended you.

The Sixth Word: It Is Consummated. O Jesus, you hung in agony on the Cross for love of me. From this tree you announced the truth of my redemption, a redemption which made us children of God and heirs of heaven. Pity all the faithful who are now facing death; pity me when I also shall be facing mine. By the merits of your precious blood, detach us from the pleasures of the world and grant us the grace to offer you the sacrifice of our life in reparation for our sins. Amen.

Have mercy on us, O Lord.

My God, I believe in you, I hope in you, I love you. I am sorry for my sins because by them I have offended you.

The Seventh Word: Father, Into Your Hands I Commend My Spirit. O Jesus, you hung in agony on the Cross for love of me. You accomplished my salvation through your full acceptance of the will of your eternal Father. You commended your spirit into his hands, bowed your head, and died. Have pity on all the faithful who are now facing death, and pity me when I too shall be facing mine. By the merits of your precious blood, give us at our last breath a complete conformity to your divine will. Make us ready to live or die as it pleases you. Let us desire nothing more than to accomplish whatever you have willed for us. Amen.

Have mercy on us, O Lord.

My God, I believe in you, I hope in you, I love you. I am sorry for my sins because by them I have offended you.

INVOCATION TO THE HOLY CROSS

The Cross is my sure salvation. The Cross I ever adore. The Cross of my Lord is with me. The Cross is my refuge. Amen.

SAINT THOMAS AQUINAS

DEVOTION IN HONOR OF THE FIVE WOUNDS OF CHRIST

I adore you, cross, in honor of the Cross on which hung our Lord Jesus Christ. By that holy wound which for our sakes you did bear in your right hand on the Cross, I pray you, Lord, to deliver me from all ills of body and soul.

Dearest Jesus, by that holy wound which you did suffer in the right foot on the Cross, lead us to know the way of truth. Glorious Jesus, by that holy wound which you bore for us in your left hand on the Cross, guard our hands from doing anything that is contrary to your will.

Blessed Jesus, by that holy wound which you received in your left foot on the Cross, keep our feet from going astray, keep them always on the path that leads to you.

Dearest Jesus, by that holy wound in your side, enkindle in our hearts the fire of your love; make us burn with unceasing longing to do your will as we ought.

O God, who for us sinners placed your hands and feet and your whole body on the Cross, and who bore the crown of thorns on your head, who suffered the five wounds for us sinners, redeeming us with your sacred blood, grant us this day and every day to practice penitence, patience, humility, and chastity; give us light, wisdom, understanding, and true knowledge, through yourself, who with the Father and the Holy Spirit lives and reigns, world without end. Amen.

PRAYER TO THE LIVING TREE OF THE CROSS

Come, you faithful, let us pay homage to the life-giving tree on which Christ of his own free will stretched out his hands in order to restore our lost blessedness. Come, you faithful, let us pay homage to the tree which has enabled us to crush the heads of our invisible enemies. Come, all of humankind, let us honor the Cross of our Lord. With reverence, we Christians greet his Cross and glorify the God who is nailed upon it. Lord, you who are nailed to the Cross, kind friend of all, have mercy on us.

Today the Lord of creation is nailed to the Cross and his side is pierced. He who brings all sweetness to us tastes gall and vinegar. He who created the heavens is crowned with a crown of thorns. He who made all creatures with his hands is clothed in a garment of mockery and struck by the hands he has made. He who rules the sky submits to the scourge, and for my sake is spat upon, whipped, and humiliated in order to save the world from sin because he is full of mercy.

Let us have before our eyes today that mighty Cross on which our Savior slew death. Let us draw near in awe and reverence and with praising lips, for all of us have received the grace of salvation through that Cross on which the sacred victim was offered.

Lord, strengthen your Church which you have acquired by virtue of your Cross. By that Cross you have vanquished the foe and brought light to all the world. Amen.

PRAYER OF RICHARD ROLLE

Lord Jesus, your body is like a net; for like a net is full of holes, so your body is full of wounds. Come, Lord Jesus, catch me in the net of your scourging, that all my heart and love may draw me ever closer to you as a net draws the fish. May no temptation or trial or prosperity ever pull me away from you; and as a net draws fish to land, bring me to the land of your eternal blessing. Catch me, Lord, in the net of the holy Church and hold me fast that I may never break out of its bonds.

Jesus, your body is a book written with red ink; so is your body all written over with blood-red wounds. Grant me, Jesus, the grace to read this book often and to understand the sweetness of its writing. Give me the grace to know the unparalleled love of Jesus Christ and to learn by that example to love God as I should. And, Jesus, grant me the grace to study this book at each moment of the day, and to find in it my mediation, my speech, and my prayer. Amen.

SEVEN OFFERINGS OF THE PRECIOUS BLOOD OF JESUS CHRIST

I. Eternal Father, I offer you the merits gained by the precious blood of your Son, Jesus Christ, for the holy Church, for the safety and well-being of her visible head, the pope, and for all those who minister in your sanctuary on earth.

Blessing and thanks be to Jesus, who with his blood has saved us.

II. Eternal Father, I offer you the merits gained by the precious blood of your Son, Jesus Christ, for peace among all nations, for the spread of our holy faith, and for the welfare of all people.

Blessing and thanks be to Jesus, who with his blood has saved us.

III. Eternal Father, I offer you the merits of the precious blood of your Son, Jesus Christ, for the repentance of all sinners and for the conversion of all those who do not yet know you.

Blessing and thanks be to Jesus, who with his blood has saved us.

IV. Eternal Father, I offer you the merits of the precious blood of your Son, Jesus Christ, for all my family, friends, and enemies; for the poor, the sick, and the suffering, and for all for whom you, my God, know that I ought to pray.

Blessing and thanks be to Jesus, who with his blood has saved us.

V. Eternal Father, I offer you the merits of the precious blood of your Son, Jesus Christ, for all who, this day, are facing death, that you would save them from hell and admit them quickly to your glory.

Blessing and thanks be to Jesus, who with his blood has saved us.

VI. Eternal Father, I offer you the merits of the precious blood of your Son, Jesus Christ, for all those who treasure this great sign of our salvation and who join with me in honoring it.

Blessing and thanks be to Jesus, who with his blood has saved us.

VII. Eternal Father, I offer you the merits of the precious blood of your Son, Jesus Christ, for all my wants, spiritual and worldly, in aid of the holy souls in purgatory, and especially for those have honored your spent blood which is the price of our redemption.

Blessing and thanks be to Jesus, who with his blood has saved us.

LITANY OF THE PRECIOUS BLOOD

Lord, have mercy.

Christ, have mercy.

Lord, have mercy.

Christ, hear us.

Christ, graciously hear us.

God, the Father of heaven, *have mercy on us.*

God the Son, Redeemer of the world, *have mercy on us.*

Holy Trinity, one God, *have mercy on us.*

Blood of Christ, only-begotten Son of the eternal Father,
     save us.

Blood of Christ, incarnate Word of God, *save us.*

Blood of Christ, of the new and eternal Testament, *save us.*

Blood of Christ, falling upon the earth in agony, *save us.*

Blood of Christ, shed profusely in the scourging, *save us.*

Blood of Christ, flowing forth in the crowning with thorns,
     save us.

Blood of Christ, poured out on the Cross, *save us.*

Blood of Christ, price of our salvation, *save us.*

Blood of Christ, without which there is no forgiveness, *save us.*

Blood of Christ, eucharistic drink and refreshment of souls,
save us.

Blood of Christ, stream of mercy, *save us.*

Blood of Christ, victor over demons, *save us.*

Blood of Christ, courage of martyrs, *save us.*

Blood of Christ, strength of confessors, *save us.*

Blood of Christ, bringing forth virgins, *save us.*

Blood of Christ, help of those in peril, *save us.*

Blood of Christ, relief of the burdened, *save us.*

Blood of Christ, solace in sorrow, *save us.*

Blood of Christ, hope of the penitent, *save us.*

Blood of Christ, consolation of the dying, *save us.*

Blood of Christ, peace and tenderness of hearts, *save us.*

Blood of Christ, pledge of eternal life, *save us.*

Blood of Christ, freeing souls from purgatory, *save us.*

Blood of Christ, most worthy of all glory and honor, *save us.*

V. You have redeemed us, O Lord, in your blood.

R. And made us, for our God, a kingdom.

Let us pray. Almighty and eternal God, you have appointed your only-begotten Son the Redeemer of the world, and willed to be appeased by his blood. Grant, we beg of you, that we may worthily adore this price of our salvation, and through its power be safeguarded from the evils of the present life, so that we may rejoice in its fruits forever in heaven. Through Christ our Lord. Amen.

2. Prayers to the Sacred Heart of Jesus

ACT OF CONSECRATION TO THE SACRED HEART

I give myself and consecrate myself to the Sacred Heart of our Lord Jesus Christ, my person and my life, my actions, pains and sufferings, so that I may be unwilling to make use of any part of my being other than to honor, love, and glorify the Sacred Heart. This is my unchanging purpose, namely, to be all his, to do all things for the love of him, at the same time renouncing with all my heart whatever is displeasing to him.

I therefore take you, O Sacred Heart, to be the only object of my love, the guardian of my life, my assurance of salvation, the remedy of my weakness and inconstancy, the atonement for all the faults of my life and my sure refuge at the hour of death. Be then, O Heart of goodness, my justification before God the Father, and turn away from me the strokes of his righteous anger.

O Heart of love, I put all my confidence in you, for I fear everything from my own wickedness and frailty, but I hope for all things from your goodness and bounty. Remove from me all that can displease you or resist your holy will; let your pure love imprint your image so deeply upon my heart, that I shall never be able to forget you or to be separated from you. May I obtain from all your loving kindness the grace of having my name written in your heart, for in you I desire to place all my happiness and glory, living and dying in bondage to you. Amen.

PROMISES OF THE SACRED HEART TO
SAINT MARGARET MARY/NINE FIRST FRIDAYS

The principal promises that the Sacred Heart of Jesus has made in favor of those who are devoted to him are as follows:

- I will give them all the graces necessary for their state in life.
- I will give peace in their families.
- I will console them in all their troubles.
- I will be their refuge in life and especially in death.
- I will abundantly bless all their undertakings.
- Sinners will find in my Heart the source and infinite ocean of mercy.
- Tepid souls will become fervent.

- Fervent souls will rise to great perfection.
- I will bless those places where the image of my Sacred Heart shall be exposed and venerated.
- I will give priests the power to touch the most hardened hearts.
- Persons who propagate this devotion will have their names eternally written in my Heart.
- In the abundant mercy of my Heart, I promise that my all-powerful love will grant to all those who will receive Communion on the first Fridays, for nine consecutive months, the grace of final repentance. They will not die in my displeasure, nor without receiving the sacraments; and my Heart will be their secure refuge in that last hour.

CARDINAL NEWMAN'S PRAYER TO THE SACRED HEART

Most sacred, most loving Heart of Jesus, you are concealed in the Holy Eucharist. I worship you with all my best love and awe, with deep affection, and with my most resolved will. For a while you take up your home within me. O make my heart beat with your Heart! Purify it of all that is earthly, all that is proud, of all perversity, and of all disorder. So fill it with you, that neither the events of the day, nor the circumstances of the time, may have the power to ruffle it; but that in your love and your fear, it may have peace. Amen.

ACT OF REPARATION TO THE SACRED HEART

Jesus, ever present on our altars, we cast ourselves at your feet, overcome with sorrow at the sight of the ingratitude which afflicts your heart.

Look on us, laden down with our own sins and with the sins of all humankind, so that by this homage, we may offer you acceptable atonement and reparation. Have mercy on us, O Jesus. From the

Cross you forgave your executioners; pardon us also. Listen to the pleadings of your Sacred Heart, and our sins will be consumed in its love.

With the fire of your love, O Jesus, destroy in us all that is displeasing to you and implant in our hearts sentiments that will appease your justice. Sacred Heart of Jesus, be the salvation of all Christians, the safeguard of those who have recourse to you, and the refuge of sinners. Grant us the grace of devoting ourselves entirely to your service, so that we may finally share in the inheritance you have reserved for those who love you. Amen.

LITANY OF THE SACRED HEART

Lord, have mercy on us. Christ, have mercy on us. Lord, have mercy on us.

Christ, hear us. Christ, graciously hear us.

God, the Father of heaven, *have mercy on us.*
God, the Son, Redeemer of the world, *have mercy on us.*
God, the Holy Spirit, *have mercy on us.*
Holy Trinity, one God, *have mercy on us.*
Heart of Jesus, Son of the eternal Father, *have mercy on us.*
Heart of Jesus, formed by the Holy Spirit in the womb of the
    Virgin Mother, *have mercy on us.*
Heart of Jesus, united to the Word of God, *have mercy on us.*
Heart of Jesus, of infinite majesty, *have mercy on us.*
Heart of Jesus, sacred temple of God, *have mercy on us.*
Heart of Jesus, tabernacle of the Most High, *have mercy on us.*
Heart of Jesus, house of God and gate of heaven,
    have mercy on us.
Heart of Jesus, burning furnace of charity, *have mercy on us.*
Heart of Jesus, vessel of justice and love, *have mercy on us.*

Heart of Jesus, full of goodness and love, *have mercy on us.*

Heart of Jesus, abyss of all virtues, *have mercy on us.*

Heart of Jesus, most worthy of all praise, *have mercy on us.*

Heart of Jesus, king and center of all hearts, *have mercy on us.*

Heart of Jesus, keeper of all the treasures of wisdom
and knowledge, *have mercy on us.*

Heart of Jesus, in whom dwells the fullness of God,
have mercy on us.

Heart of Jesus, in whom the Father was well pleased,
have mercy on us.

Heart of Jesus, of whose fullness we have all received,
have mercy on us.

Heart of Jesus, desire of the everlasting hills,
have mercy on us.

Heart of Jesus, patient and most merciful, *have mercy on us.*

Heart of Jesus, enriching all who invoke you, *have mercy on us.*

Heart of Jesus, fountain of life and holiness, *have mercy on us.*

Heart of Jesus, propitiation for our sins, *have mercy on us.*

Heart of Jesus, loaded down with opprobrium, *have mercy on us.*

Heart of Jesus, bruised for our offenses, *have mercy on us.*

Heart of Jesus, obedient unto death, *have mercy on us.*

Heart of Jesus, pierced with a lance, *have mercy on us.*

Heart of Jesus, source of all consolation, *have mercy on us.*

Heart of Jesus, our life and resurrection, *have mercy on us.*

Heart of Jesus, victim for sin, *have mercy on us.*

Heart of Jesus, salvation of those who trust in you,
have mercy on us.

Heart of Jesus, hope of those who die in you, *have mercy on us.*

Heart of Jesus, delight of all the saints, *have mercy on us.*

Lamb of God, who takes away the sins of the world, spare us, O Lord.

Lamb of God, who takes away the sins of the world, hear us, O Lord.

Lamb of God, who takes away the sins of the world, have mercy on us.

V. Jesus, meek and humble of heart,
R. Make our hearts like unto yours.

Let us pray. Almighty and eternal God, look upon the heart of your dearly beloved Son, and on the praise and satisfaction he offers you in the name of sinners who seek your mercy. Be appeased and grant us pardon in the name of the same Jesus Christ, your Son, who lives and reigns with you in the unity of the Holy Spirit, world without end. Amen.

PRAYER OF TRUST IN THE SACRED HEART

In all my temptations, I place my trust in you,
O Sacred Heart of Jesus.
In all my weaknesses, I place my trust in you,
O Sacred Heart of Jesus.
In all my difficulties, I place my trust in you,
O Sacred Heart of Jesus.
In all my trials, I place my trust in you,
O Sacred Heart of Jesus.
In all my sorrows, I place my trust in you,
O Sacred Heart of Jesus.
In all my work, I place my trust in you,
O Sacred Heart of Jesus.
In every failure, I place my trust in you,
O Sacred Heart of Jesus.
In every discouragement, I place my trust in you,
O Sacred Heart of Jesus.

In life and in death, I place my trust in you,
    O Sacred Heart of Jesus.
In time and eternity, I place my trust in you,
    O Sacred Heart of Jesus.

3. Prayers to the Holy Name of Jesus

PRAYER TO THE HOLY NAME

O Jesus, grant to me and those I love as well, as to all the faithful, the grace of eternal salvation through your holy Name.

Bestow on us a deep and abiding love for you that will imprint your holy Name upon our hearts.

May it always be in our minds and frequently on our lips that it may be our defense in temptation, our refuge in danger, and our consolation in the hour of our death. Amen.

LITANY OF THE HOLY NAME OF JESUS

Lord, have mercy on us.
Christ, have mercy on us.
Lord, have mercy on us.

Jesus, hear us.
Jesus, graciously hear us.

God the Father of heaven, *have mercy on us.*
God the Son, Redeemer of the world, *have mercy on us.*
God the Holy Spirit, *have mercy on us.*
Most Holy Trinity, one God, *have mercy on us.*
Jesus, Son of the living God, *have mercy on us.*
Jesus, splendor of the Father, *have mercy on us.*
Jesus, brightness of eternal light, *have mercy on us.*
Jesus, King of glory, *have mercy on us.*

Jesus, son of justice, *have mercy on us.*

Jesus, Son the Virgin Mary, *have mercy on us.*

Jesus, most amiable, *have mercy on us.*

Jesus, most admirable, *have mercy on us.*

Jesus, the mighty God, *have mercy on us.*

Jesus, the Father of the world to come, *have mercy on us.*

Jesus, the Angel of great counsel, *have mercy on us.*

Jesus, most powerful, *have mercy on us.*

Jesus, most patient, *have mercy on us.*

Jesus, most obedient, *have mercy on us.*

Jesus, meek and humble of heart, *have mercy on us.*

Jesus, lover of chastity, *have mercy on us.*

Jesus, lover of us, *have mercy on us.*

Jesus, the God of peace, *have mercy on us.*

Jesus, the Author of life, *have mercy on us.*

Jesus, the example of virtues, *have mercy on us.*

Jesus, the zealous lover of souls, *have mercy on us.*

Jesus, our God, *have mercy on us.*

Jesus, our refuge, *have mercy on us.*

Jesus, the father of the poor, *have mercy on us.*

Jesus, the treasure of the faithful, *have mercy on us.*

Jesus, the good shepherd, *have mercy on us.*

Jesus, the true light, *have mercy on us.*

Jesus, infinite goodness, *have mercy on us.*

Jesus, our way and our life, *have mercy on us.*

Jesus, the joy of angels, *have mercy on us.*

Jesus, the king of patriarchs, *have mercy on us.*

Jesus, the master of the apostles, *have mercy on us.*

Jesus, the teacher of the Evangelists, *have mercy on us.*

Jesus, the strength of martyrs, *have mercy on us.*

Jesus, the light of confessors, *have mercy on us.*

Jesus, the purity of virgins, *have mercy on us.*
Jesus, the crown of all saints, *have mercy on us.*

Be merciful unto us, *spare us, O Lord Jesus.*
Be merciful unto us, *hear us, O Lord Jesus.*
From all evil, Jesus, *deliver us.*
From all sin, Jesus, *deliver us.*
From your wrath, *deliver us.*
From the snares of the devil, *deliver us.*
From everlasting death, *deliver us.*
From the neglect of your inspirations, *deliver us.*
Through the mystery of your holy Incarnation, *deliver us.*
Through your Nativity, *deliver us.*
Through your infancy, *deliver us.*
Through your most divine life, *deliver us.*
Through your labors, *deliver us.*
Through your agony and passion, *deliver us.*
Through your Cross, *deliver us.*
Through your sufferings, *deliver us.*
Through your death and burial, *deliver us.*
Through your Resurrection, *deliver us.*
Through your Ascension, *deliver us.*
By the most holy institution of your Eucharist, *deliver us.*
Through your joys, *deliver us.*
Through your glory, *deliver us.*
Lamb of God, who takes away the sins of the world,
    Jesus, spare us.
Lamb of God, who takes away the sins of the world,
    Jesus, graciously hear us.
Lamb of God, who takes away the sins of the world,
    have mercy on us.

Jesus, hear us.

Jesus, graciously hear us.

Let us pray. O Lord Jesus Christ, who has said: Ask, and you shall receive; seek, and you shall find; knock, and it will be opened to you; grant, through the gift of your most divine love, our most humble supplications, the gift of your most divine love, that we may ever love you with our whole hearts, words, and works, and never cease praising you.

O Lord, give us a perpetual fear as well as love of your most holy Name, for you never cease to help those who love you. Amen.

PRAYER TO THE HOLY NAME

O God, who appointed your only-begotten Son to be the Savior of humankind and who commanded his name to be called Jesus, mercifully grant that we may enjoy the company of him in heaven, whose holy Name we venerate on earth. Through the same Christ our Lord. Amen.

PRAISE OF THE HOLY NAME

Jesus, O name full of glory, grace, love, and strength, you are the refuge of those who repent, our banner in the conduct of this life, the medicine of souls, the comfort of those who mourn, the garland of those who believe, the light of those who seek the truth, the wages of those who toil, the healing of those who are sick. To you we send our hopes; by you our prayers are heard. We delight to contemplate your most holy Name, O Jesus, you who are the glory of the saints for all eternity. Amen.

SAINT BERNARDINE OF SIENA

4. Prayers to the Child Jesus

PRAYER TO THE INFANT JESUS

Lord, you graciously allowed your divinity to be incarnated in your most sacred humanity, so as to be born in time and as a little child. We acknowledge your infinite wisdom displayed in the silence of a child, your power disguised as weakness, and your majesty veiled in humiliation. As we venerate your humiliations on earth, may we also contemplate your glories in heaven, who with the Father and the Holy Spirit, live and reign forever and ever. Amen.

FIVE OFFERINGS OF THE CHILD JESUS

I. Eternal Father, I offer to your honor and glory, and for my own salvation, and for the salvation of all the world, the mystery of the birth of our divine Savior. Glory be to the Father, and to the Son, and to the Holy Spirit. Amen.

II. Eternal Father, I offer to your honor and glory, and for my eternal salvation, the sufferings of the holy Virgin and of Saint Joseph on that journey from Nazareth to Bethlehem; I offer you their pain in finding no place to shelter themselves when the Savior of the world was about to be born. Glory be to the Father, and to the Son, and to the Holy Spirit. Amen.

III. Eternal Father, I offer to your honor and glory, and for my eternal salvation, the stable where Jesus was born, the harsh straw which served him for a bed, the swaddling clothes which bound him, and his tender infant cries. Glory be to the Father, and to the Son, and to the Holy Spirit. Amen.

IV. Eternal Father, I offer to your honor and glory, and for my eternal salvation, the poor manger, the sign of poverty, in which he chose to lay his infant limbs. Glory be to the Father, and to the Son, and to the Holy Spirit. Amen.

V. Eternal Father, I offer to your honor and glory, and for my eternal salvation, humility, patience, charity, and all the virtues of the Child Jesus; I thank you and I bless you for this ineffable mystery of the Incarnation of the divine Word. Glory be to the Father, and to the Son, and to the Holy Spirit. Amen.

V. The Word was made flesh.
R. And dwelt among us.

Let us pray. O God, whose only-begotten Son was made manifest to us in the substance of our flesh, grant, we beseech you, that our souls may be inwardly renewed through him, who is externally like ourselves, who lives and reigns with you forever and ever. Amen.

LITANY OF THE INFANT JESUS

Lord, have mercy.
Christ, have mercy.
Lord, have mercy.

Jesus, hear us.
Jesus, graciously hear us.

God, the Father of heaven, *have mercy on us.*
God, the Son, Redeemer of the world, *have mercy on us.*
God, the Holy Spirit, *have mercy on us.*
Holy Trinity, one God, *have mercy on us.*

Infant, Jesus Christ, *have mercy on us.*
Infant, true God, *have mercy on us.*
Infant, Son of the living God, *have mercy on us.*
Infant, Son of the Virgin Mary, *have mercy on us.*
Infant, strong in weakness, *have mercy on us.*
Infant, powerful in tenderness, *have mercy on us.*
Infant, treasure of grace, *have mercy on us.*
Infant, fountain of love, *have mercy on us.*
Infant, renewer of the heavens, *have mercy on us.*
Infant, repairer of the evils of the earth, *have mercy on us.*
Infant, head of the angels, *have mercy on us.*
Infant, root of the patriarchs, *have mercy on us.*
Infant, speech of prophets, *have mercy on us.*
Infant, desire of the Gentiles, *have mercy on us.*
Infant, joy of shepherds, *have mercy on us.*
Infant, light of the Magi, *have mercy on us.*
Infant, salvation of infants, *have mercy on us.*
Infant, expectation of the just, *have mercy on us.*
Infant, instructor of the wise, *have mercy on us.*

Be merciful, *spare us, O Infant Jesus.*
Be merciful, *graciously hear us, O Infant Jesus.*
From the slavery of the children of Adam, Infant Jesus, *deliver us.*
From the evil desires of the flesh, Infant Jesus, *deliver us.*
From the malice of the world, Infant Jesus, *deliver us.*
From the pride of life, Infant Jesus, *deliver us.*
From the inordinate desire of knowing, Infant Jesus, *deliver us.*
From the blindness of spirit, Infant Jesus, *deliver us.*
From an evil will, Infant Jesus, *deliver us.*
From our sins, Infant Jesus, *deliver us.*
Through your most pure Conception, Infant Jesus, *deliver us.*
Through your most humble Nativity, Infant Jesus, *deliver us.*

Through your tears, Infant Jesus, *deliver us.*
Through your Circumcision, Infant Jesus, *deliver us.*
Through your most glorious Epiphany, Infant Jesus, *deliver us.*
Through your most pious Presentation, Infant Jesus, *deliver us.*
Through your most divine life, Infant Jesus, *deliver us.*
Through your poverty, Infant Jesus, *deliver us.*
Through your many sufferings, Infant Jesus, *deliver us.*
Through your labors and travels, Infant Jesus, *deliver us.*

Lamb of God, you take away the sins of the world, have mercy on us,
    O Infant Jesus.
Lamb of God, you take away the sins of the world, graciously hear us,
    O Infant Jesus.
Lamb of God, you take away the sins of the world, have mercy on us,
    O Infant Jesus.

V. Jesus, Infant, hear us. *R.* Jesus, Infant, graciously hear us.

5. Prayers for Divine Mercy

CHAPLET OF DIVINE MERCY

Recite one Our Father, one Hail Mary, and the Apostles' Creed. Then, on the single beads between the ten beads of the rosary, say the following:
Eternal Father, I offer you the body and blood, soul and divinity of your dearly beloved Son, our Lord Jesus Christ, in atonement for our sins and for those of the whole world.

On the ten beads or decades of the rosary, say these words:
For the sake of his sorrowful passion, have mercy on us and on the whole world.

At the conclusion of each decade, recite the following prayer three times:
Holy God, Holy Mighty One, Holy Immortal One, have mercy on us and on the whole world.

PRAYER FOR DIVINE MERCY

O merciful God, great fount of goodness, today all people call out to you from the depths of their misery for your saving mercy. They call out for your compassion, O God, with a mighty voice of misery: gracious God, do not reject the prayers of these earthly exiles! O Lord, goodness beyond our understanding, who is acquainted with our misery through and through and who knows that we cannot ascend to you by our own power, we implore you, anticipate us with your grace and keep on increasing your mercy in us, that we may faithfully do your holy will all through our life and at the hour of our death.

Let the power of your mercy shield us from the arrows of our enemies, that we may with confidence, as your children, await your final coming—that day which is known to you alone. And we expect to obtain everything promised us by Jesus in spite of all our wretched sinfulness. For Jesus is our hope: through his merciful heart as through an open gate we pass on to heaven. Amen.

SISTER MARIA FAUSTINA

6. Prayers to the Holy Eucharist

ORDER OF EXPOSITION OF THE EUCHARIST AND BENEDICTION OF THE BLESSED SACRAMENT

The aim of this devotion is to acknowledge Christ's presence in the Sacrament, remembering that this presence is expressed most fully in the holy sacrifice of the Mass. This form of adoration is directed toward spiritual communion and a deeper dwelling with the Lord in the holy Eucharist. This service consists of songs, readings, and prayers, along with appropriate eucharistic hymns.

Exposition: Exposition of the Eucharist begins with the priest approaching the altar while the people sing a song. The priest makes an appropriate reverence and then removes the Sacrament from the place of reservation, and places it (in the ciborium or monstrance) on the altar. If the monstrance is used, the priest incenses the Sacrament.

Adoration: A reading of Scripture followed by a period of silence occurs next. To encourage a better understanding of the mystery of the holy Eucharist, a homily may be given. If the exposition of the Blessed Sacrament is rather lengthy, part of the Liturgy of the Hours may also be offered to God as part of the celebration. It is especially appropriate to use the liturgy of the hours. A eucharistic hymn, such as the following, may be sung.

> O Saving Victim, opening wide
> The gate of heav'n to us below!
> Our foes press on from every side:
> Your aid supply, your strength bestow.
>
> To your great name be endless praise,
> Immortal Godhead, One in Three;
> O grant us endless length of days
> When our true native land we see.
> SAINT THOMAS AQUINAS

Benediction: At the end of the eucharistic adoration, the priest goes to the altar. As a eucharistic song, such as the one that follows, is sung, the priest, kneeling, incenses the Sacrament.

> Down in adoration falling,
> Lo! the sacred Host we hail;
> Lo! o'er ancient forms departing,
> Newer rites of grace prevail;

Faith for all defects supplying,
Where the feeble senses fail.

To the everlasting Father
And the Son who reigns on high,
With the Holy Spirit proceeding
Forth from each eternally,
Be salvation, honor, blessing,
Might, and endless majesty. Amen.

SAINT THOMAS AQUINAS

The people respond when the priest says or sings the following versicle:

V. You have given them bread from heaven.
R. Having all sweetness within it.

The priest continues with the following prayer, one of seven prescribed options:

Lord, Jesus Christ, you have given us this sacrament
in remembrance of your suffering and death.
May our worship of this sacrament of your body and blood
help us to experience the salvation you have won for us
and the peace of the kingdom where you live
with the Father and the Holy Spirit,
one God, forever and ever.
All: Amen.

After the prayer, the priest takes the monstrance (or ciborium) and makes the Sign of the Cross over the people in silence. The priest then places the Eucharist back in the tabernacle. He makes the ap-

propriate reverence and returns to the sacristy while the people sing
a hymn (or recite an acclamation), such as the following:

> Holy God, we praise your name!
> Lord of all, we bow before you;
> All on earth your scepter claim,
> All in heav'n above adore you;
> Infinite is your vast domain,
> Everlasting is your reign.

> Hark! The loud celestial hymn
> Angel choirs above are raising;
> Cherubim and Seraphim
> In unceasing chorus praising,
> Fill the Heav'ns with sweet accord;
> Holy, holy, holy Lord.

DIVINE PRAISES

Blessed be God.
Blessed be his holy name.
Blessed be Jesus Christ, true God and true man.
Blessed be the name of Jesus.
Blessed be his Sacred Heart.
Blessed be his most precious blood.
Blessed be Jesus in the most holy Sacrament of the altar.
Blessed be the Holy Spirit, the Paraclete.
Blessed be the great Mother of God, Mary most holy.
Blessed be her holy and Immaculate Conception.
Blessed be her glorious Assumption.
Blessed be the name of Mary, virgin and mother.
Blessed be Saint Joseph, her most chaste spouse.
Blessed be God in his angels and his saints. Amen.

3. Prayer for a Visit to the Blessed Sacrament

Lord Jesus Christ, who, through the love you bear to us, remains with us day and night in the Blessed Sacrament, full of mercy and love, expecting, inviting, and receiving all who come to visit, I believe that you are present in the Sacrament of the altar. I adore you and I thank you for all the favors which you have bestowed on me, particularly for having given yourself to me in this sacrament, for having given me for my advocate your most holy Mother Mary, and for having called me to visit you in this church.

I salute your most loving heart, and I do this for three ends: first, in thanksgiving for this great gift; second, in compensation for all the injuries you have received in this sacrament; and third, I wish by this visit to adore you and offer you company in all those places where you are least honored and most abandoned in the holy sacrament. My Jesus, I love you with my whole heart. I am sorry for having offended your infinite goodness. I propose, with the help of your grace, never more to offend you; and, at this moment, as miserable as I am, I consecrate my whole being to you. I give you my entire will, all my affections and desires, and all that I have.

From this day forward, do what you wish with me, and whatever belongs to me. I ask only for your holy love, the gift of final perseverance, the accomplishment of your will. I recommend the souls in purgatory to you, particularly those who were most devoted to the Blessed Sacrament and to our most holy Mary. I also recommend to you all poor sinners. Finally, my dear Savior, I unite all my affections with the affections of your most loving heart; and thus united, I offer them to your eternal Father, and I beg him, in your name, and for your sake, to accept them.

SAINT ALPHONSUS LIGUORI

ACT OF SPIRITUAL COMMUNION

My Jesus, I believe that you are truly present in the most Blessed Sacrament. I love you above all things and I desire to possess you within my soul. Since I am unable now to receive you sacramentally, come at least spiritually into my heart. I embrace you as being already there, and unite myself wholly to you. Never, never permit me to be separated from you.

SAINT ALPHONSUS LIGUORI

PRAYER OF NICOLAS OF CUSA

O Lord, how sweet is your goodness. It is your will that we proclaim your death in the eating of the Bread of Life. What more could you give to us, who deserve to die through the eating of the forbidden fruit than life through the eating of the Bread? O Food of Life, nailed to the Cross, who can grasp the bountiful gift which you offer—the gift of your very self as food? Here is generosity beyond all measure, when the giver and the gift are one and the same.

O Food which truly nourishes and satisfies, not our flesh but our soul, not our body but our spirit. O Memorial, worthy to be cherished in our inmost soul, to be deeply engraved on our mind, and lovingly preserved in the tabernacle of our heart. Its remembrance is a joy forever, and a cause for tears that well up from a heart filled with overpowering joy. Amen.

LITANY OF THE BLESSED SACRAMENT

Lord, have mercy.
Christ, have mercy.
Lord, have mercy.
Christ, hear us.
Christ, graciously hear us.
God the Father of heaven, *have mercy on us.*

God, the Holy Spirit, *have mercy on us.*

Holy Trinity, one God, *have mercy on us.*

Living Bread, that came down from heaven, *have mercy on us.*

Hidden God and Savior, *have mercy on us.*

Corn of the elect, *have mercy on us.*

Wine whose fruit are virgins, *have mercy on us.*

Bread of fatness, and royal delicacies, *have mercy on us.*

Perpetual Sacrifice, *have mercy on us.*

Clean Oblation, *have mercy on us.*

Lamb without spot, *have mercy on us.*

Most pure Feast, *have mercy on us.*

Food of Angels, *have mercy on us.*

Hidden Manna, *have mercy on us.*

Memorial of the wonders of God, *have mercy on us.*

Supersubstantial Bread, *have mercy on us.*

Word made flesh, dwelling in us, *have mercy on us.*

Sacred Host, *have mercy on us.*

Mystery of faith, *have mercy on us.*

Most high and adorable Sacrament, *have mercy on us.*

Most holy of all sacrifices, *have mercy on us.*

True Propitiation for the living and the dead, *have mercy on us.*

Heavenly Antidote against the poison of sin, *have mercy on us.*

Most wonderful of all miracles, *have mercy on us.*

Most holy commemoration of the passion of Christ,
    have mercy on us.

Gift transcending all fullness, *have mercy on us.*

Special memorial of divine love, *have mercy on us.*

Affluence of divine bounty, *have mercy on us.*

Most august and holy mystery, *have mercy on us.*

Medicine of immortality, *have mercy on us.*

Tremendous and life-giving sacrament, *have mercy on us.*

Bread made flesh by the omnipotence of the Word,
have mercy on us.
Unbloody sacrifice, *have mercy on us.*
Our feast at once and our fellow-guest, *have mercy on us.*
Sweetest banquet, at which angels minister, *have mercy on us.*
Sacrament of piety, *have mercy on us.*
Bond of charity, *have mercy on us.*
Priest and victim, *have mercy on us.*
Spiritual sweetness tasted in its proper source, *have mercy on us.*
Refreshment of holy souls, *have mercy on us.*
Viaticum of those who die in the Lord, *have mercy on us.*
Pledge of future glory, *have mercy on us.*

Be merciful, *spare us, O Lord.*
Be merciful, *graciously hear us, O Lord.*
From an unworthy reception of your body and blood,
O Lord, deliver us.
From the lust of the flesh, *O Lord, deliver us.*
From the lust of the eyes, *O Lord, deliver us.*
From the pride of life, *O Lord, deliver us.*
From every occasion of sin, *O Lord, deliver us.*
Through the desire by which you desired to eat this Passover
with your disciples, *O Lord, deliver us.*
Through the profound humility by which you washed their feet,
O Lord, deliver us.
Through that ardent charity by which you instituted
this divine sacrament, *O Lord, deliver us.*
Through your precious blood which you have left us on our altars,
O Lord, deliver us.
Through the five wounds of this your most holy body
which you received for us, *O Lord, deliver us.*
We sinners, *we beseech you, hear us.*

That you would preserve and increase our faith, reverence,
and devotion toward this sacrament, *we beseech you, hear us.*
That you would conduct us, through a true confession of our sins,
to a frequent reception of the holy Eucharist,
we beseech you, hear us.
That you would deliver us from all heresy, evil,
and blindness of heart, *we beseech you, hear us.*
That you would impart to us the precious and heavenly fruits
of this most holy sacrament, *we beseech you, hear us.*
That at the hour of death you would strengthen and defend us
by this heavenly Viaticum, *we beseech you, hear us.*

Son of God, Lamb of God, you take away the sins of the world,
spare us, O Lord.
Lamb of God, you take away the sins of the world,
graciously hear us, O Lord.
Lamb of God, you take away the sins of the world,
have mercy on us, O Lord.
Christ, hear us.
Christ, graciously hear us.
V. You gave them bread from heaven,
R. Containing in itself all sweetness.

Let us pray. O God, in this wonderful sacrament you left us a memorial of your passion. Grant us so to venerate the sacred mysteries of your body and blood that we may ever continue to feel within us the blessed fruit of your redemption. You live and reign forever and ever. Amen.

PRAYER FROM THE COPTIC LITURGY

We thank you, O Lord our God, the true Word, who has loved us and thus gave us yourself as a sacrifice for our redemption, who has granted us life from your holy body and precious blood, and who has made us worthy to partake of them. We confess our sins to you, O God, lover of your creatures, and send up to you glory and honor and worship with the Father and the Holy Spirit, now and forever. Amen.

PRAYER OF SAINT JOHN CHRYSOSTOM

O Lord, bless those who bless you, and sanctify those who trust in you, save your people and bless their inheritance, and keep your household the Church under your protection. Sanctify those who love the beauty of your house; reward them with glory through your divine power; and do not forsake those who hope in you. To the sick give your aid, healing, and comfort. Keep safe all who travel by land or water. Send us seasonable weather and bless the fruits of the earth. Keep peace in the world, and among all your people. Grant rest to the departed, and remember those who have offered gifts to you. Save those who are in any way afflicted or distressed, and grant us all your heavenly grace. Amen.

SECTION SIX

Prayers to the Holy Spirit and the Blessed Trinity

1. Prayers to the Holy Spirit

PRAYER TO THE HOLY SPIRIT

O Holy Spirit, let your finger touch me, your finger that drops down wine and oil and the choicest myrrh. Let your finger touch me, most beloved Lord, and when it has rid me of corruption, let it restore my wholeness, so that, when you come to dwell in me, you may find me not a thoroughfare, nor a bag with holes, but a dwelling intact and entire, founded on the truth of faith, erected in the certainty of hope, and completed in the zeal of charity.

Come, most welcome guest, knock, and enter into my soul. Open the door, and let no one shut it. Enter, and close the door behind you. For all the things that you possess are in peace, and there is no peace apart from you. You are indeed rest for those that toil, peace for those that strive, bliss for those who grieve, comfort for the weary, coolness for the fevered, merriment for mourners, light for those in darkness, and courage for those who are afraid. What more is there to say? You are all good. Amen.

PRAYER FOR THE GIFT OF FEAR

Open your generous hand that fills all that has breath and blessing, and give me the gift of fear, which counters temptations of the flesh. Bounteously fill me with fear, so that, fearing future perils, I may draw near to God.

Be to me as two feet, the right imbued with longing to be joined to God, the left filled with desire to flee the occasions of sin. Direct my goings according to your word, so that each foot follows the other, advancing each in turn with an even tread. For in this way, my progress will be straight, turning neither to the right or to the left.

This fear is the beginning of wisdom. Lacking this fear, our first parents did not recoil from the tasteless fruit, but stood, and looked, and touched, and tasted, yet did not find the taste for which they had hoped, but rather only bitterness. O true Sweetness, I have stood and looked and touched and tasted in disobedience to your word as often as I have taken food or breath. If this is the way of my life, correct me, for I am dying by living in this way. I imagine that I am living by it, yet it is death to me.

Give me, O Holy Spirit, your gift of fear. Deliver me from evil. It is evil only that makes slaves, so to be freed from evil is to be made free. O Spirit Liberator, deliver us from this slavery, and increase the goodness in us through the holiness of your spirit. Amen.

PRAYER FOR THE GIFT OF KNOWLEDGE

Holy Spirit, give yourself to me so that I may distinguish evil from evil, wrong from wrong, and what hurt each one does. Grant me, Spirit of knowledge, the blessing of this gift. This spirit makes a person mindful of the past, wary about the future, and guarded in the present. It brings forth honey from the rock. It turns difficult things to pleasantness, pains to delight, and sins to profit. It is a lantern that illuminates your ways, O Lord, a light for my path; without it, everyone who walks the road of repentance goes astray. This is the spirit that rescued Israel from slavery in Egypt and freed Joseph from prison. To Job it gave back gifts of many kinds. It made Moses the friend of God.

But see! When the enemy who is set against the human race sees that no resistance is being offered, he wages another war in the hope of victory. He stirs up pride, urges revenge, and provokes scorn, so that in this way he may overcome us. Though he promises strength, weakness is the prize that he gives. Against this enemy, O Sweetness of the Lord, give us the gift of knowledge, that by union with the Word of God, we may have the power to stand firmly and resist strongly. Amen.

PRAYER FOR THE GIFT OF UNDERSTANDING

O most sweetest of teachers, give your Spirit to me so that I will direct my energies to work along with you. May your spirit direct this activity so that it may serve the kingdom of God and that I may be submissive to his requests. If I knew my own heart, I would desire to be ruled rather than to rule, for I would be able to see how truly weak I am. Bestow on me, then, this grace, which is called the spirit of understanding. Let it teach me to know myself so that I may desire subjection and not authority. Send me your understanding, O Lord, the Paraclete, that it may guide my understanding, not downwards, but upwards from which it came. Lift up my eyes so that I will see that to be ruled by the King above is better than to rule some lower things.

To be ruled by him is to rule; he reigns, who is the servant of so great a King. Come, then, Spirit of Understanding, come and cleanse my heart in penitence, so that its enlightened eyes may see your will. Grant that I will keep your law in all things, for they are profitable, they lead to life. Most Holy Spirit of Understanding, make me like a little child, pure in heart, so that by holy gazing I may enjoy the sight of God. Amen.

PRAYER FOR FULFILLMENT BY THE HOLY SPIRIT

Come, most gracious Spirit, come. Come, Mercy beyond all words and Grace beyond all comparing. Come, everlasting Fire, Dove unchangeable. Come down, in pity, and never leave us, inbreathe, inpour yourself to fill and enliven us with your spirit. You are our union, your are our Uniter. Let your fire join and keep us joined. Feed your new chicks, most holy Dove, and lead them forth. Lead them through to that eternal nest, where with God the Father and the Son you abide for all eternity. Amen.

PRAYER FOR THE FRUITS OF THE SPIRIT

O Bounteous Spirit, I ask you to bring forth in my life your fruits: the fruit of love, so I may love you above all things and all others for your sake; the fruit of joy, that I may find my delight in your service; the fruit of peace, that I may be pardoned through your mercy and may rest in your love; the fruit of long-suffering so that I may bear, with patience, all afflictions; the fruit of gentleness, that I may subdue all anger and take calmly and sweetly all trials and provocations; the fruit of meekness, that I may forgive freely all who have hurt me and endure with patience all burdens that are laid upon me; the fruit of temperance that I may restrain all my desires and bring them into the subjection of your holy will. Amen.

NOVENA FOR PENTECOST

O Holy Spirit of God, take me as your disciple, guide me, illuminate me, sanctify me. Bind my hands that I may do no evil; cover my eyes that I may not see it; sanctify my heart so that evil may not rest within me. Be my Guide! Wherever you lead, I will go; whatever you command, I will do.

O Holy Spirit, come into my heart. By your power, draw me to you and grant me charity with fear. Guard me from every evil thought; warm me with your sweetest love so that all pain may seem light to me. Help me now in every action.

O Holy Spirit, infinite love of the Father and the Son, I offer myself this day and all the days of my life to you, O Consuming Fire. I am now firmly resolved more than ever to hear your voice and to do all things in compliance with your holy will. Amen.

2. Prayers to the Blessed Trinity

PRAYER OF PRAISE TO THE HOLY TRINITY

Praise to you, O Lord, who in the beginning created us in freedom. Praise to you, O Lord, who endowed us with reason and free will.

Praise to you, O Just Father, who in your love has desired to have us for your very own.

Praise to you, O Holy Son, who for our salvation did put on a human body like ours.

Praise to you, O Spirit of Life, who has enriched us with your gifts.

Praise to you, O Lord, who has brought us to know your divinity.

Praise to You, Lord, who has made us worthy to join with the angels in praising you.

From every mouth, let praise rise up to you, Father, Son, and Holy Spirit. On the heights and in the depths, let there be praise to the Holy Trinity, on earth and in heaven, from the beginning to the end of time, world without end. Amen.

SAINT SYMEON THE NEW THEOLOGIAN

PRAYER IN HONOR OF THE BLESSED TRINITY

O eternal Trinity, I have seen that I am in your image and likeness. Eternal Father, you have granted me a share in your own power and given to my understanding that wisdom which comes only from your only-begotten Son, while the Holy Spirit, proceeding from you and your Son, made my will capable of loving you. You, eternal Trinity, you are the Creator and I am your creature. My soul continually hungers after you, desiring to see you with the light of your light. As the deer desires the springs of living water, so my soul desires to leave this dark body and see you in truth.

O unfathomable Abyss! You are the fire that consumes all self-love in the soul, the fire which melts all ice and which gives all light.

113

You are the fire that takes away cold. With your light, you illuminate me so that I may know your truth. Clothe me with yourself, eternal truth, so that I may live this moral life with true obedience, and with the light of your most holy faith. Amen.

SAINT CATHERINE OF SIENA

GAELIC PRAYER TO THE TRINITY

I am bending my knee in the eye of the Father
   who created me,
In the eye of the Son who purchased me,
In the eye of the Spirit who cleansed me,
In friendship and affection.
Through your own Anointed One, O God,
Bestow upon us fulfillment of our need,
Love toward God,
The affection of God,
The smile of God,
The wisdom of God,
The grace of God,
The fear of God,
And the will of God,
To do in the world of the Three,
As angels and saints
Do in heaven;
Each shade and light,
Each day and night,
Each time in kindness,
Give us your spirit.
Amen.

Prayers to the Blessed Virgin Mary

1. Traditional Prayers to Our Lady

WE FLY TO YOUR PROTECTION OR *SUB TUUM*

We fly to your protection,
O holy Mother of God;
despise not our petitions
in our necessities,
but deliver us always from all danger,
O glorious and blessed Virgin.
Amen.

MEMORARE

Remember, O most gracious Virgin Mary,
that never was it known
that anyone who fled to your protection,
implored your help, or sought your intercession
was left unaided.
Inspired with this confidence,
I fly to you, O Virgin of virgins, my Mother.
To you I come,
before you I stand, sinful and sorrowful.
O Mother of the Word Incarnate,
despise not my petitions,
but in your mercy, hear and answer me.
Amen.

MAGNIFICAT

My spirit proclaims the greatness of the Lord,
my spirit finds joy in God my savior,
For he has looked upon his servant in her lowliness;
all ages to come shall call me blessed.

God who is mighty has done great things for me,
holy is his name;
His mercy is from age to age
on those who fear him.
He has shown might with his arm;
he has confused the proud in their inmost thoughts.

He has deposed the mighty from their thrones
and raised the lowly to high places.
The hungry he has given every good thing;
while the rich he has sent away empty.
He has upheld Israel his servant,
ever mindful of her mercy;
Even as he promised our fathers,
promised Abraham and his descendants forever.

LUKE 1:46–55

HAIL, HOLY QUEEN OR *SALVE REGINA*

Hail, holy Queen, Mother of Mercy; hail our life, our sweetness, and our hope. To you do we cry, poor banished children of Eve. To you do we send up our sighs, mourning and weeping in this valley of tears. Turn, then, most gracious advocate, your eyes of mercy toward us. And after this our exile show unto us the blessed fruit of your womb, Jesus, O clement, O loving, O sweet Virgin Mary.

QUEEN OF HEAVEN OR *REGINA COELI*

Queen of heaven, rejoice, alleluia.
For he whom you merited to bear, alleluia.
Has risen as he said, alleluia.
Pray for us to God, alleluia.
Rejoice and be glad, O Virgin Mary, alleluia.
Because the Lord is truly risen, alleluia.

Let us pray: O God, who by the Resurrection of your Son, our Jesus Christ, granted joy to the whole world, grant, we beg of ̣ ̣ ̣, that through the intercession of the Virgin Mary, his Mother, we may lay hold of the joys of eternal life, through the same Christ, our Lord. Amen.

LITANY OF THE BLESSED VIRGIN MARY OR LITANY OF LORETO

Lord, have mercy. Christ, have mercy.

Lord, have mercy. Christ, hear us.

Christ, graciously hear us.

God, the Father of heaven, have mercy on us.

God, the Holy Spirit, have mercy on us.

Holy Trinity, one God, have mercy on us.

Holy Mary, *pray for us.*

Holy Mother of God, *pray for us.*

Holy Virgin of virgins, *pray for us.*

Mother of Christ, *pray for us.*

Mother of divine grace, *pray for us.*

Mother most pure, *pray for us.*

Mother most chaste, *pray for us.*

Mother inviolate, *pray for us.*

Mother undefiled, *pray for us.*

Mother most amiable, *pray for us.*

Mother most admirable, *pray for us.*

Mother of good counsel, *pray for us.*

Mother of our Creator, *pray for us.*

Mother of our Savior, *pray for us.*

Virgin most prudent, *pray for us.*

Virgin most venerable, *pray for us.*

Virgin most renowned, *pray for us.*

Virgin most powerful, *pray for us.*

Virgin most merciful, *pray for us.*

Virgin most faithful, *pray for us.*
Mirror of justice, *pray for us.*
Seat of wisdom, *pray for us.*
Cause of our joy, *pray for us.*
Spiritual vessel, *pray for us.*
Vessel of honor, *pray for us.*
Singular vessel of devotion, *pray for us.*
Mystical rose, *pray for us.*
Tower of David, *pray for us.*
Tower of ivory, *pray for us.*
House of gold, *pray for us.*
Ark of the Covenant, *pray for us.*
Gate of Heaven, *pray for us.*
Morning star, *pray for us.*
Health of the sick, *pray for us.*
Refuge of sinners, *pray for us.*
Comforter of the afflicted, *pray for us.*
Help of Christians, *pray for us.*
Queen of angels, *pray for us.*
Queen of patriarchs, *pray for us.*
Queen of prophets, *pray for us.*
Queen of apostles, *pray for us.*
Queen of martyrs, *pray for us.*
Queen of confessors, *pray for us.*
Queen of virgins, *pray for us.*
Queen of all saints, *pray for us.*
Queen conceived without original sin, *pray for us.*
Queen assumed into heaven, *pray for us.*
Queen of the most holy rosary, *pray for us.*
Queen of peace, *pray for us.*

Lamb of God, who takes away the sins of the world, spare us, O Lord.

Lamb of God, who takes away the sins of the world, graciously hear us, O Lord.

Lamb of God, who takes away the sins of the world, have mercy on us, O Lord.

Pray for us, O holy Mother of God, that we may be made worthy of the promises of Christ.

Let us pray: Grant, we beseech you, O Lord God, that we your servants may enjoy perpetual health of mind and body and by the glorious intercession of the Blessed Mary, ever Virgin, be delivered from present sorrow and enjoy eternal happiness. Through Christ, our Lord. Amen.

2. Prayers of the Saints to Mary

PRAYER OF SAINT VENANTIUS

O holy Flower of David, most blessed Virgin Mary: You have brought forth for us the long-awaited Emmanuel. You are the Holy City, founded by God himself, O Virgin worthy of all praise. You are, O matchless one, she whom God has laden with all the riches of the universe, the true Tree of Life, planted in the midst of Paradise, from whose branches do not hang the fruit of sin, but the food of immortality.

Hail, Queen, clothed with the sun, for whose feet the moon is a footstool, whose crown is set with the stars of heaven, hail, Mother, who became for fallen peoples the Gate of Paradise. Hail, Glory of Heaven, Splendor of God, first Fruit of our reclamation, fairest Creature of the hand of God.

You are more beautiful than the rose, purer than the lily, more spotless that the fallen snow. You shine with greater glory than the radiant sun. You are above all angels and saints. You are the Child of Grace who has given the children of Eve eternal life by giving them your Son.

O loving Mother: commend us to your Son; for every prayer from you is honorable. Through the praise we give you, obtain for us our goal of heaven, where we will rejoice in your glory for all eternity. Amen.

INVOCATIONS TO THE BLESSED VIRGIN MARY

O Mary, Mother of God!
You are the honored Dwelling Place.
Through my prayers make of me
A chosen vessel to receive
The blessing of your Son!

O Blessed Mother of God,
Open the gate of compassion
To us whose hope is in you,
That we may not be confused,
But be preserved from adversity, through you,
Who are the salvation of all Christian folk.

O Full of Grace!
You are the joy of all creation,
Of the assembly of the angels
and of the whole human race.
You, holy Temple, spiritual Paradise,
boast of maidenhood, by whom God took Flesh,
When he, who exists as God
Before the worlds were made, became a child.
He made your womb his throne,
and he enlarged your heart broader than the heavens.

O Steadfast Protectress of Christians,
Constant advocate of the Creator,
Do not ignore the cry of the sinful,
But out of your goodness be ready to help us
Who call on you with all confidence.

Make haste to hear our petitions!
Make haste to intercede for us,
O Mother of God,
Who ever and always protects those who give honor to you.
Amen.

SAINT JOHN CHRYSOSTOM

PRAYER TO THE MOTHER OF GOD

Hail, O Mary, Mother of God,
Virgin and Mother! Morning Star, perfect vessel.
Hail, O Mary, Mother of God,
Holy Temple in which God himself was conceived.
Hail, O Mary, Mother of God,
Chaste and pure dove.
Hail, O Mary, Mother of God,
Who enclosed the one who cannot be encompassed
    in your sacred womb.
Hail, O Mary, Mother of God,
From you flowed the true light, Jesus Christ, our Lord.
Hail, O Mary, Mother of God,
Through you the Conqueror and triumphant Vanquisher of hell
    came to us.
Hail, O Mary, Mother of God,
Through you the glory of the Resurrection blossoms.
Hail, O Mary, Mother of God,
You have saved every faithful Christian.

Holy Mary, Mother of God,
Pray for us sinners now and at the hour of our death.
Amen.

SAINT CYRIL OF ALEXANDRIA

SALUTATION TO THE BLESSED VIRGIN

We salute you, most pure Virgin; we beg you to receive our loving greetings.

Rejoice, O Mother of him who is eternal joy. Be happy, you who augmented the happiness of heaven.

Who can speak worthily of your greatness; you are the ornament of our human nature. You are more beautiful than all other creatures; for in your purity, you surpass them all. We call you, therefore, "full of grace."

You are united with the Lord more closely than are the angels and the saints. You alone are his Mother. What mind can measure the height of your glory or the abundance of your merits?

Therefore, we, your servants, never tire of repeating, "Hail, full of grace. The Lord is with you. Blessed are you among women." You changed the curse of our first mother to a blessing, for through you the blessing of the Lord came down upon the earth once more, blotting out the traces of the first curse. You alone, O Virgin most blessed, were worthy to become the Mother of the Eternal Word, from you was formed the New Adam, Jesus Christ. Amen.

TO THE BLESSED VIRGIN MARY FOR THE GIFT OF THANKFULNESS

O Spouse of God, who sits at his right hand, clothed with gold and gems, place the mantle of divine pardon on us whose every grace and gift was despoiled by the curse of original sin. O unconquered Virgin, who crushed the serpent with your foot, hail, O most immaculate abode of the King of Heaven, you are raised on humility and holiness. May the loving devotion of our prayers be pleasing to you; may our prayers which give thanks to God for your many privileges make us also grateful to you. Receive, then, our prayers: present them to your Son, so that he may grant us the favor of eternal happiness through you. Amen.

TO THE IMMACULATE VIRGIN FOR PURITY

O Mary, Virgin before the divine birth, guard my body and soul. Hail Mary, full of grace, the Lord is with you. Blessed are you among women, and blessed is the fruit of your womb, Jesus. Holy Mary, Mother of God, pray for us sinners now and at the hour of our death. Amen.

TO OUR SORROWFUL LADY

O holy Virgin, Mother of our Lord Jesus Christ, by the grief that you experienced when you witnessed the martyrdom, the crucifixion, and the death of your divine Son, look on me with the eyes of compassion, awaken in my heart a sincere abhorrence of my sins. Help me to disengage from all undue affection for the passing joys of earth, so that I may long only for the eternal Jerusalem, and center all my thoughts and actions toward this one most desirable object. Honor, glory, and love to our divine Lord Jesus and to the holy and immaculate Mother of God. Amen.

PRAYER OF SAINT JOHN OF THE CROSS

Most holy Mary, Virgin of virgins, shrine of the most Holy Trinity, joy of the angels, sure refuge of sinners, take pity on our sorrows, mercifully accept our sighs, and appease the wrath of your most holy Son. Amen.

CARDINAL NEWMAN'S GREETING TO MARY

Hail, star of the sea! You are truly a star, O Mary. Jesus Christ is himself the brightest morning star, who was prefigured by the star that appeared to the wise men of the East. Jesus is the light of the world, illuminating every one who comes into it, opening our eyes with the gift of faith, making souls luminous by his almighty grace. Mary is the Star shining with the light of Jesus, fair as the moon, and special as the sun, the star of the heavens which is good to look upon, the star of the sea which is welcome to the storm-tossed, at whose smile the evil spirit flies, and passions are hushed, and peace is poured out on the soul.

Hail, then, Star of the Sea, we are joyful in the recollection of you. Pray for us ever at the throne of grace. Plead our cause, pray with us, present our prayers to your Son now and at the hour of our death. Mary, be our help. Amen.

PRAYER TO MARY FOR AN INCREASE IN FAITH

Hail, Mary, queen of mercy, olive-branch of forgiveness, through whom we receive the medicine that heals our sickness, the balsam of pardon; Virgin Mother of the divine offspring, through your Son, your only Child who stooped to become the brother of humankind, you are the true Mother of us all. For the sake of his love, take me, unworthy as I am, into your motherly care. Sustain, preserve, and enlighten my conversion. Be for me for all eternity my cherished mother, tenderly caring for me throughout my earthly life, and enfolding me in your arms at the hour of my death. Amen.

SAINT GERTRUDE THE GREAT

PRAYER OF SAINT ALPHONSUS LIGUORI

My sorrowful Mother, by the merit of that grief which you felt at seeing your beloved Jesus led to death, obtain for me the grace to bear with patience those crosses which God sends me. I will be fortunate if I also shall know how to accompany you with my cross until death. You and Jesus, both innocent, have borne a heavy cross; and shall I, a sinner who has merited hell, refuse mine? Immaculate

Virgin, I hope you will help me to bear my crosses with patience. Amen.

CONSECRATION OF SAINT LOUIS DE MONTFORT TO MARY

I, (*Name*), faithless sinner, renew and ratify the vows of my baptism. I renounce Satan, his pomps and works; and I give myself entirely to Jesus Christ, the Incarnate Wisdom, to carry my cross after him all the days of my life, and to be more faithful to him than I have ever been before.

In the presence of all the heavenly court, I choose you this day for my mother and queen. I deliver and consecrate to you my body and soul, my goods, both interior and exterior, and even the value of all my good actions, past, present, and future. I leave to you the entire and full right of disposing of me, and all that belongs to me, without exception, according to your good pleasure, for the greater glory of God, in time and in eternity. Amen.

PRAYER OF SAINT ROBERT BELLARMINE

Virgin, adorned and clothed with the sun, come to my aid. Most beautiful, Mystical Rose, take up your home in my heart. Most pure and undefiled, grant me true peace. Deserving of all honor and praise, give me your love.

Elect and full of grace, lead me to God. Star of the Sea, dispel the storms besetting me. Most holy and sweet lady, guide me on the way. With your burning light, enlighten my mind. My lady, more precious than jewels, make reparation for me and make me more pleasing to your Son. Innocent of any sin or fault, make me more worthy of God. Enriched with every grace and gift, obtain remission of my sins. Most pure, lead me to the joys of heavenly love.

Virgin, a lily among thorns, I ask you for the grace of a happy death. More rare than the rarest dream, bring joy to my heart, most true, loving mother, Virgin Mary. Amen.

PRAYER OF SAINT ALOYSIUS GONZAGA

O holy Mary, my mistress, into your blessed trust and special custody, and into the grasp of your mercy I, this day, every day, and in the hour of my death, commend my soul and my body. To you I commit all my anxieties and miseries, my life and the end of my life, that by your most holy intercession and by your merits all my actions may be directed toward and disposed of according to your will and that of your Son. Amen.

3. Prayers to Mary Under Her Special Titles

TO OUR LADY OF GUADALUPE

O Virgin of Guadalupe, Mother of the Americas, we pray to you to lead the faithful along the paths of an intense Christian life, and of humble service to God and to other souls. Grant to our homes the grace of loving and respecting life in its beginnings, with the same love with which you conceived in your womb the life of the Son of God. Protect our families so they may always be united, and bless the upbringing of our children.

Immaculate Virgin, Mother of the Church, look upon us with compassion, teach us to go continually to Jesus and, if we fall, help us to rise again and return to him, by means of the confession of our sins in the sacrament of penance, which gives peace to the soul. Thus, with the peace of God, keep our hearts free from evil and hatred, and allow us to find eternal joy with your Son, our Lord Jesus Christ, who with God the Father and the Holy Spirit, lives and reigns forever and ever. Amen.

NOVENA PRAYER TO OUR LADY OF PERPETUAL HELP

O Mother of Perpetual Help, behold at your feet a wretched sinner who trustfully turns to you. Mother of Mercy, have pity on me. I hear all people call you the refuge and hope of sinners. Be then my refuge and my hope. Help me for the love of Jesus Christ; hold out your hand to one who is forever at your service. Praise and thanks be to God, who in his great mercy has given me this trust in you, sure pledge of my eternal salvation.

It is only too true that in the past I have fallen miserably, because I did not turn to you. I know that with your help I will conquer. I know that you will help me if I commend myself to you. But I fear that in the occasions of sin I may forget to call upon you and so be lost. This, then, is the grace I ask of you; for this I implore you with all my heart and soul: that in the assaults of hell I may ever run to your protection and say to you: Help me, Mary; Mother of Perpetual Help, let me not lose my God. Amen.

TO OUR LADY OF GOOD COUNSEL

Glorious Virgin, chosen by the eternal Wisdom to be the Mother of the eternal Word in the flesh, you who are the treasurer of God's graces and the advocate of sinners, I turn to you. Guide and counsel me in this valley of tears. Obtain for me, through the precious blood of your divine Son, the forgiveness of my sins, the salvation of my soul, and the means to bring it about. Obtain also for your holy Church the spread of the kingdom of Jesus Christ over the whole earth. Amen.

PRAYER TO OUR LADY, QUEEN OF PEACE

Most loving Mother, you who by your motherhood earned a share in your divine Son's kingship, we, your devoted children, are comforted by the thought that our Redeemer was proclaimed by the prophets and by the angels at Bethlehem as the King of Peace. Thus, it must be pleasing and acceptable to you to hear yourself greeted as the Queen of Peace, a title that comes from the very depths of our being.

May your powerful intercession keep your people from hatred and discord, and turn their hearts into the ways of peace and brotherhood, which Jesus came to teach and establish for the prosperity and safety of all.

Glorious queen, be pleased to crown with success the fatherly care with which the supreme pontiff, vicar on earth of your divine Son, strives to bring nations together and keep them united around the one and only center, the living Father. Enlighten us and our leaders so that we may not thwart his saving purposes. Revive and maintain harmony in our families, peace in our hearts, and charity throughout the world. Amen.

TO MARY, QUEEN OF THE ANGELS

Majestic Queen of the angels, you received from God the power to crush the head of Satan; therefore, we beg you, send forth the legions of heaven, that under your commission they may search out all evil spirits, engage them in battle, and hurl them back into the pit of hell.

O good and tender Mother, you will ever be our hope and the object of our love. Send for the holy angels to defend me and drive all cruel foes far from me. Holy angels and archangels, defend us, keep us safe. Amen.

TO OUR LADY, HOPE OF CHRISTIANS

Hail Mary, hope of Christians, hear the prayer of one who loves you, honors you in a special way, and places in you the hope of salvation. I owe you my life, for you obtain for me the grace of your Son and you are the sure pledge of my eternal happiness.

I beg you, deliver me from the burden of my sins, take away the darkness of my mind, destroy the earthly affections of my heart, defeat the temptations of my enemies, and rule all the actions of my life. With you as my guide, may I arrive at the eternal happiness of heaven.

SAINT JOHN DAMASCENE

PRAYER TO OUR LADY OF LOURDES

O Immaculate Virgin Mary, you are the refuge of sinners, the health of the sick, and the comfort of the afflicted. By your appearances at the Grotto of Lourdes you made it a special sanctuary where your favors are given to those who visit it from around the world. Over the years, many have received a cure for their sufferings—whether of soul, mind, or body. Therefore, I come to you with enormous confidence to ask your motherly intercession. Loving Mother, obtain for me the granting of my requests. Let me strive to imitate your virtues on earth so that I may one day share your glory in heaven. Amen.

TO OUR LADY OF MOUNT CARMEL

O beautiful flower of Carmel, most fruitful vine, splendor of heaven, who brought forth the Son of God while still remaining a virgin, assist me in my need. O Star of the Sea, help and protect me! Show me that you are my Mother. O Mary, conceived without sin, pray for us. O most Immaculate Mary! Watch over your own child, and obtain my request from Almighty God. Mother and Ornament of Carmel, pray for us. Amen.

TO OUR LADY OF FÁTIMA

Beloved Mother, most holy Virgin, Our Lady of Fátima, we acknowledge with sadness the suffering of your immaculate heart, surrounded as it is with the thorns ungrateful people have placed around your heart. Moved by our love of you as our Mother, we place ourselves at your feet and humbly want to make reparations to you by means of our prayers and sacrifices for the grievances you have suffered.

Speak on our behalf, Fairest Lady, and obtain for us pardon of our sins and grace to make amends for them. Hasten the conversion of all peoples so that they may learn to love the Lord. Turn your eyes of mercy toward us, so that we may love God with all our hearts while on earth and enjoy his presence forever in heaven. Amen.

NOVENA PRAYER TO OUR LADY OF PERPETUAL HELP

Our Lady of Perpetual Help, you are the dispenser of every grace that God grants to us in our misery; this is why he has made you so powerful, so rich, and so kind. You are the advocate of the most unfortunate and abandoned sinners, if they but come to you. Come once more to my assistance, for I commend myself to you. In your hands I place my eternal salvation; to you I entrust my soul. Enroll me among your most faithful servants.

Take me under your protection and it is enough for me. For if you protect me, I shall fear nothing—not my sins, for you will obtain for me their pardon and remission; not the evil spirits, for you are mightier than all the powers of hell; not even Jesus, my judge, for he is appeased by a single prayer from you.

I fear only that through my own negligence I may forget to recommend myself to you and so I will be lost. My dear Lady, obtain for me the forgiveness of my sins, love for Jesus, final perseverance, and the grace to have recourse to you at all times. Amen.

NOVENA PRAYER TO OUR LADY OF THE MIRACULOUS MEDAL

O Immaculate Virgin Mary, Mother of our Lord Jesus and our Mother, filled with the most lively confidence in your all-powerful and never-failing intercession, manifested so often through the Miraculous Medal, we your loving and trustful children implore you to obtain for us the graces and favors we ask during this novena, if they will be beneficial to our immortal souls, and the souls for whom we pray. (*Here privately mention your petition.*) You know, O Mary, how often our souls have been the sanctuaries of your Son, who hates sinfulness. Obtain for us, then, a deep hatred of sin, and that purity of heart that will attach us to God alone, so that our every thought, word, and deed, may tend to his greater glory. Obtain for us also a spirit of prayer and self-denial, that we may recover by penance what we have lost by sin, and at length attain to that blessed abode, where you are the Queen of Angels and of all human beings. Amen.

4. Devotions to Our Blessed Virgin

OBSERVANCE OF THE FIVE CONSECUTIVE FIRST SATURDAYS

This observance was requested to be introduced to the Church by the Blessed Virgin during one of her appearances at Fátima in 1917. This devotion can be practiced individually or as a group. The observances requested by Our Lady of Fátima are practiced as follows:

1. Make a good confession and receive holy Communion on each of five consecutive first Saturdays of the month.
2. Recite five decades of the rosary, adding at the end the Fátima prayer taught to the children by Our Lady herself: O My Jesus, forgive us our sins, deliver us from the fires of hell, draw the souls of all to heaven, especially those in greatest need.
3. Keep Mary company for fifteen minutes while meditating on the fifteen mysteries of the rosary with the intention of making reparation for sins.
4. Conclude with a recitation of the following prayer:

Immaculate Heart of Mary, full of love of God and all people, I consecrate myself entirely to you. I entrust to you the salvation of my soul. With your help may I hate sin, love God and my neighbor, and reach eternal life together with those whom I love.

Mediatrix of Grace and Mother of Mercy, your divine Son has merited boundless treasures of grace by his sufferings, which he has confided to you for us, your children. Filled with confidence in your Motherly Heart, I come to you with my pressing needs. For the sake

133

of the Sacred Heart of Jesus, obtain for me the favor I ask. (*Here mention your request.*)

Dearest Mother, if what I ask for should not be according to God's will, pray that I may receive that which will be of greater benefit to my soul. May I experience the kindness of your motherly heart and the power of your intercession with Jesus during life and at the hour of my death.

V. Immaculate Heart of Mary,
R. Pray for us, who have recourse to you.

Let us pray: O God of infinite goodness and mercy, fill our hearts with a great confidence in our most holy Mother, whom we invoke under the title of the Immaculate Heart of Mary, and grant us by her most powerful intercession all the graces, spiritual and temporal, which we need. Through Christ our Lord. Amen.

DEVOTION OF THE THREE HAIL MARYS

This devotion, also called "A Little Key to Heaven," consists simply of saying three Hail Marys each day, usually in the morning and at night, to obtain a happy death. This devotion arose from a vision to Saint Matilde of Hacehborn, Germany, of Our Lady, who said to her, "I have a little key that will open the door of heaven for you when you die. All you have to do is to say, in my honor, three Hail Marys, every day."

THE ROSARY OF SAINT DOMINIC

This rosary is composed of fifteen decades, divided into three parts, each containing five decades. The first part consists of five joyful events in the life of Jesus and Mary, the second part recalls five sorrowful events, and the third part considers five glorious events.

We begin by making the Sign of the Cross.

Then we say the Apostles' Creed, one Our Father, three Hail Marys, and one Glory Be on the beads of the shorter chain. Then we recall the first mystery, say one Our Father, ten Hail Marys, and one Glory Be. This completes one decade. All the other decades are said in the same manner, with a different mystery meditated upon during each decade. At the end of the rosary, the prayer Hail, Holy Queen may be recited.

The mysteries of the rosary are scenes from the lives of Jesus and Mary. By meditating on these sublime truths, we come to a better understanding of our faith: the Incarnation of the Lord, the Redemption, and the Christian life—present and future. The following are the mysteries of the rosary. The Scripture quotations listed in parentheses that follow each mystery can be used as a basis for meditating on that particular event. A suggested intention is given within the second set of parentheses.

THE JOYFUL MYSTERIES

1. The Annunciation (Luke 1:26–38) (For the love of humility)
2. The Visitation (Luke 1:39–56) (For charity toward one's neighbor)
3. The Birth of Christ (Luke 2:1–19) (For the spirit of poverty)
4. The Presentation (Luke 2:22–40) (For the virtue of obedience)
5. The Finding in the Temple (Luke 2:41–52) (For the virtue of piety)

THE SORROWFUL MYSTERIES

1. The Agony in the Garden (Luke 22:39–46) (For true contrition)
2. The Scourging at the Pillar (John 19:1–3) (For the virtue of purity)
3. The Crowning With Thorns (Matthew 27:27–31) (For moral courage)

4. The Carrying of the Cross (Matthew 27:32) (For the virtue of patience)

5. The Crucifixion (Matthew 27:35–50) (For final perseverance)

THE GLORIOUS MYSTERIES

1. The Resurrection (Mark 16:1–14)(For the virtue of faith)
2. The Ascension (Luke 24:50–53) (For the virtue of hope)
3. The Descent of the Holy Spirit (Acts 2:1–12) (For the love of God)
4. The Assumption of Mary into Heaven (Judith 13:23–31) (For devotion to Mary)
5. The Coronation of the Blessed Virgin Mary (Revelation 12) (For eternal happiness)

FIFTEEN PROMISES OF MARY TO THOSE WHO RECITE THE ROSARY

These promises were given by Our Lady in an apparition to Saint Dominic and Alan de la Roche:

1. Whoever recites the rosary shall receive singular graces.
2. I promise special protection to those who recite the rosary.
3. The rosary will destroy vice, decrease sin, and defeat heresies.
4. The rosary will cause virtue and good works to flourish; it will obtain for souls the abundant mercy of God; it will withdraw the hearts of people from the love of the world and all its vanities, and will lift them to the desire of those things that are eternal.
5. The souls of those who recite the rosary shall not perish.
6. Those who recite the rosary devoutly shall never be conquered by misfortune. God will not chastise them in his justice; they shall not perish by an unprovided death; if they are just, they shall remain in the grace of God and become worthy of eternal life.

7. Those who have a true devotion to the rosary shall not die without the sacraments of the Church.

8. Those who are faithful in the recitation of the rosary shall have, during their life and at their death, the light of God and the plenitude of his graces; at the moment of death, they shall participate in the merits of the saints in paradise.

9. I shall deliver from purgatory those who have been devoted to the rosary.

10. The faithful children of the rosary shall merit a high degree of glory in heaven.

11. You shall obtain all that you ask of me by the recitation of the rosary.

12. All those who propagate the holy rosary shall be aided by me in their necessities.

13. I have obtained from my divine Son that all the advocates of the rosary shall have for intercessors the entire celestial court during their life and at the hour of death.

14. All who recite the rosary are my children, and brothers and sisters of my only Son, Jesus Christ.

15. Devotion to my rosary is a sign of predestination.

GROUP OR FAMILY ROSARY

The rosary can be fruitfully said by an assembly, either a family or a prayer group. In this case, the saying of the rosary may be preceded by a Scripture reading, an introductory prayer, and a hymn. Silence is often observed between the decades as an opportunity for further meditation. The rosary is concluded by a spontaneous or summarizing prayer. The meditations for each decade may be given by a different member of the group, as may the function of the prayer leader alternate among those present.

PRAYER BEFORE THE FAMILY ROSARY

Most Holy Trinity, Father, Son, and Holy Spirit, we, the members of this family, place ourselves under your protection. Through the mysteries of the rosary may we know your plan of salvation and learn how much you love us. May your kingdom come in our family so that we may one day share in your heavenly home hereafter. Amen.

PRAYER AFTER THE FAMILY ROSARY

Holy Mary, Mother of God, be a mother to each one in this home. As in Cana you watched over the needs of a married couple, watch now over the needs of this family. And as you stood by the cross of your Son and saw him die, stand by each one of us, father, mother, children, and lead us at the hour of death to our true home in heaven. Amen.

THE FRANCISCAN CROWN OR THE ROSARY (CHAPLET) OF THE SEVEN JOYS

Devotion to the Seven Joys or Seven Delights of Mary was encouraged by the Franciscans as far back as their founding in the thirteenth century. Saint Bernardine of Siena (d. 1444) and his followers promoted this devotion as the Chaplet of the Seventy-two Hail Marys.

This devotion is often used as a seven-decade rosary in which each joy is meditated on during the recitation of each decade of Hail Marys. At the end of the rosary, two Hail Marys are added in order to commemorate the traditional seventy-two years of Mary's life. These are followed by the Our Father, the Hail Mary, and a Glory Be. One form of the Seven Joys of Our Lady is as follows:

1. The Annunciation by the angel Gabriel
2. Mary's visit to her cousin Elizabeth
3. The birth of Christ

4. The adoration of the Magi
5. Finding Jesus in the Temple
6. The Resurrection of Christ
7. The Assumption of Mary into heaven

THE ROSARY (CHAPLET) OF THE SEVEN SORROWS
OF THE BLESSED VIRGIN MARY

Devotion to the Seven Sorrows of Mary probably originated under the influence of the Dominican order and Blessed Henry Suso (d. 1366) in the fourteenth century. It spread throughout the Church and seemed to have reached its present form in 1482 under the influence of a parish priest of Flanders, John de Coudenberghe. The Seven Sorrows of Mary are as follows:

1. The prophecy of Simeon (Lk 2:34–35)
2. The flight into Egypt (Mt 2:13–21)
3. The loss of the boy Jesus for three days (Lk 2:41–50)
4. The way of the Cross (Jn 19:17)
5. The crucifixion and death of Christ (Jn 19:18–30)
6. Jesus taken down from the Cross (Jn 19:38)
7. Jesus laid in the tomb (Jn 19:42)

The Seven Sorrows of Mary can be prayed as a seven-decade rosary during which each of Mary's sorrows is meditated on as the ten Hail Marys of each decade are prayed. This rosary is preceded by an act of contrition asking for true sorrow for sins. Each set of Hail Marys is interspersed with an Our Father, an additional Hail Mary, and a Glory Be. It is concluded by three additional Hail Marys in memory of the tears of our Blessed Virgin and this closing prayer:

O Mother, pray that my love may rest with you and your Son, our Savior, who shed his blood for my salvation. May the memory of your sorrows abide in my own soul, so that my heart may burn with love for you and your Son. To him be honor, glory, and thanksgiving forever and ever. Amen.

FOUR GRACES GIVEN TO THOSE WHO ARE DEVOTED TO OUR LADY OF SORROWS

According to Saint Alphonsus Liguori, the following four special graces were revealed by Christ to Saint Elizabeth of Hungary and are granted to those devoted to the Seven Sorrows:

1. Those who before death invoke the Blessed Mother under the name of her Seven Sorrows will obtain true repentance for all of their sins.
2. Christ will protect all those devoted to Our Lady of Sorrows in all their trials and especially at the hour of death.
3. Christ will impress on the minds of all those devoted to Our Lady of Sorrows the memory of his passion.
4. Christ will commit those devoted to Our Lady of Sorrows into the hands of Mary, so that she might obtain for them all the graces she wishes to lavish on them.

THE SCAPULAR

The scapular has its origins in a medieval cloak or apron worn by monks and nuns as part of their religious garb. Gradually, lay people became affiliated with various religious orders and adopted aspects of their religious practice. The long piece of cloth which hung down in front and back with a hole in the center for the head—the scapular—became an outward sign of this affiliation on the part of lay people. In time, a stylized scapular—two small decorated squares of cloth connected by two pieces of ribbon or cord—came into use. There are eight Marian scapulars approved by the Church:

1. The white Scapular of the Hearts of Jesus and Mary
2. The blue Scapular of the Immaculate Conception
3. The white Scapular of the Immaculate Heart of Mary
4. The white Scapular of Our Lady of Good Counsel
5. The white Scapular of Our Lady of Ransom
6. The black Scapular of our Lady of Sorrows
7. The green "Scapular" of Our Lady
8. The brown Scapular of Our Lady of Mount Carmel

The last named, the brown scapular, is perhaps the oldest and most widely practiced of the scapular devotions to Our Lady. Often ornamented with pictures, it originated in a vision of Our Blessed Virgin to Saint Simon Stock, an English Carmelite. In this vision, Our Lady showed him a large scapular and gave it to him as a sign of great blessings for his order of Carmelites. She promised that whoever died wearing it would not suffer everlasting punishment and would quickly be released from purgatory. This grace is known as the Sabbatine Privilege. The scapular, in its cloth or medal form, may be worn by anyone as a visible sign of commitment to Marylike service and of a desire to receive protection from Our Lady.

PRAYER SEQUENCE COMMEMORATING
THE PRIVILEGES OF OUR LADY

In the name of the Father and of the Son and of the Holy Spirit. Amen.

O God, come to my assistance.

O Lord, make haste to help me.

Glory be to the Father, and to the Son, and to the Holy Spirit. Amen.

Hail to you, purest, holiest Mother of Jesus. We humbly pray you, by your predestination, whereby you were even from all eternity elected

Mother of God; by your Immaculate Conception, whereby you were conceived without stain of original sin; by your most perfect resignation, whereby you were ever conformed to the will of God; and, lastly, by your consummate holiness, whereby throughout your whole life you never committed one single fault: we pray you to become our advocate with our Lord, that he may pardon our many sins, which are the cause of his wrath. And you, O Father Almighty, by the merits of these privileges vouchsafed to this your well-beloved Daughter, hear her Supplications for us and pardon us, her children.

Spare, O Lord, spare your people. (*Say one Our Father, one Hail Mary, and one Glory Be.*)

By your holy and Immaculate Conception deliver us, glorious Virgin Mary.

Hail to you, purest, holiest Mother of Jesus. We humbly pray you, by the most holy Annunciation, when you conceived the divine Word in your womb; by your most happy delivery, in which you experienced no pain; by your perpetual virginity, which you did unite with the fruitfulness of a mother; and, lastly, by the bitter martyrdom which you underwent upon the Savior's death: we pray you to become our mediatrix, that we may reap the fruit of the precious blood of your Son. And you, O divine Son, by the merit of these privileges granted to your well-beloved Mother, hear her supplications, and pardon us, her children.

Spare, O Lord, spare your people. (*Say one Our Father, one Hail Mary, and one Glory Be.*)

By your holy and Immaculate Conception deliver us, glorious Virgin Mary.

Hail to you, purest, holiest Mother of Jesus. We humbly pray you, by the joys which you felt in your heart at the Resurrection and Ascension of Jesus Christ; by your Assumption into heaven, whereby you were exalted above all the Choirs of the Angels; by the glory which God has given to you as Queen of All Saints; and, lastly, by that most powerful intercession, whereby you are able to obtain all that you desire: we pray you, obtain for us true love of God. And you, O Holy Spirit, by the merits of these privileges of your well-beloved Spouse, hear her supplications, and pardon us, her children. Amen.

Spare, O Lord, spare your people. (*Say one Our Father, one Hail Mary, and one Glory Be.*)

By your holy and Immaculate Conception deliver us, O glorious Virgin Mary.

Antiphon: Your conception, Virgin Mother of God, brought joy to the whole world, for of you was born the Sun of Justice, Christ our God, who, loosing the curse, bestowed the blessing, and, confounding death, gave unto us eternal life.

V. In your Conception, Virgin Mary, you were Immaculate.
R. Pray to the Father for us, whose Son Jesus, conceived by the Holy Spirit, you brought forth. Let us pray.

God of mercy, God of pity, God of tenderness, who, pitying the affliction of your people, said to the angel smiting them, "Withhold your hand"; for the love of your glorious Mother, at whose precious breast you found an antidote to the venom of our sins, bestow on us the help of your grace, that we may be freed from all evil, and mercifully protected from every onset of destruction. Who lives and reigns forever and ever. Amen.

Prayers for Personal Needs and Particular Groups

1. Prayers for Personal Needs

IN DEPRESSION

O God, you care for your creation with great tenderness. In the midst of overwhelming pain, you offer hope. Give help to me, whose spirit seems to be lost and whose soul is in despair. Let me feel your love. Let me believe in a rebirth of joy so that I can experience now a small taste of the happiness I wish to know in eternity. Amen.

DIMMA, AN IRISH MONK

TO DESIRE NOTHING BUT GOD

Let us desire nothing else, let nothing else please us and cause us delight except our Creator and Redeemer, the one, true God, who is the fullness of good, the true and supreme good who alone is merciful and gentle, delectable and sweet, who alone is holy, just, and true, who alone is kind, innocent, and pure, from whom and through whom is all pardon, all grace, and all glory of the penitent and the just, and of the blessed who rejoice together in heaven.

Therefore, let nothing hinder us, nothing separate us, and nothing come between us. Let all of us, wherever we are, in every place, at every hour, at every time of day, believe truly and humbly and keep ever in our hearts all love, honor, praise, blessing, glory, and exaltation for the Creator and Savior of all who believe in him and who is without beginning and without end, unchangeable, blessed, and totally desirable above all else forever. Amen.

SAINT FRANCIS OF ASSISI

FOR LOST TIME

Late have I loved you, O beauty so ancient and so new. Too late have I loved you! You were within me while I had gone outside to seek you. Unlovely myself, I fell heedlessly upon all those lovely things you had made. And always you were with me, and I was not with you. And all these beauties that held me far from you would not have existed unless they had their being in you.

You called, you cried, you broke open my deafness. You blazed, you gleamed, you drove away my blindness. You sent your fragrance, and I drew in my breath, and I long for you.

I tasted, and now I hunger and thirst. You touched me, and now I burn with desire for your peace. Amen.

SAINT AUGUSTINE

FOR CALM HOPE

Lord our God, great, eternal in glory, who keeps his promises to those who love him with their whole heart. You who are the life of all, the help of those who flee to you, the hope of those who cry unto you, cleanse us from our sins, secret and open, and from every thought displeasing to your goodness. Cleanse our bodies and souls, our hearts and our consciences, that with a pure heart and a clear soul, with perfect love and calm hope, we may confidently pray to you. Amen.

FOR CONFORMANCE OF MY WILL TO GOD'S

O Lord, let me not henceforth desire health or life, except to spend them for you, with you, and in you. You alone know what is good for me; do, therefore, what seems best to you. Give to me, or take from me; conform my will to yours; and grant that, with humble and perfect submission, and in holy confidence, I may receive the orders of your eternal providence; and may equally adore all that comes to me from you. Amen.

BLAISE PASCAL

FOR DISCERNMENT

Grant me, O Lord, to know what I ought to know, to love what I ought to love, to praise what delights you most, to value what is precious in your sight, to hate what is offensive to you.

Do not allow me to judge according to the sight of my eyes, nor to pass sentence according to the hearing of the ears of ignorant people; but to discern with a true judgment between things visible and spiritual, and, above all things, always to ask what is the good pleasure of your will. Amen.

THOMAS À KEMPIS

FOR FORGIVENESS OF SINS

Forgive me, O Lord, my sins, the sins of my youth, and my present sins, the sins that my parents cast upon me, original sin, and the sins that I cast upon others in an ill example; actual sins which are manifest to all the world, and sins which I have so labored to hide from the world that now they are hid from my own conscience, and my own memory. Forgive me my crying sins, and my whispering sins. Let me be but so blessed, and I shall envy no one's blessedness. Amen.

JOHN DONNE

FOR A FATHER'S LOVING CORRECTION

Have mercy on us, O Lord, and hasten not to let us be consumed in our own misery, but free us by your loving mercy. Set yourself not to mark what is done amiss but to pardon our failings.

O Lord, may we feed the hand that heals and does not wound, that cherishes and does not strike, that you may so afflict us with suffering in this life that you save us from punishment in the life to come.

With a father's pity, correct your sons and daughters; teach them, and in your great goodness give to all people peace in their days. Amen.

MOZARABIC LITURGY

FOR A GENTLE LIFE

Teach me, my Lord, to be kind and gentle in all the events of life; in disappointments, in the thoughtlessness of others, in the insincerity of those I trusted, in the unfaithfulness of those on whom I relied. Let me put myself aside, to think of the happiness of others, to hide my pains and heartaches, so that I may be the only one to suffer from them.

Teach me to profit by the suffering that comes across my path. Let me use it so that it may mellow me, not embitter me; that it may make me patient, not irritable; that it may make me broad in my forgiveness, not narrow, proud, and overbearing.

May no one be less good for having come within my influence. No one less pure, less true, less kind, less noble for having been a fellow traveler in our journey toward eternal life. As I go my rounds from one task to another, let me say, from time to time, a word of love to you, my Lord. May my life be lived in the supernatural, full of power for good, and strong in its purpose of sanctity. Amen.

FOR HUMILITY: A LITANY

O Jesus, meek and humble of heart, *hear me.*
From the desire of being esteemed, *deliver me, O Jesus.*
From the desire of being loved, *deliver me, O Jesus.*
From the desire of being extolled, *deliver me, O Jesus.*
From the desire of being honored, *deliver me, O Jesus.*
From the desire of being praised, *deliver me, O Jesus.*
From the desire of being preferred to others, *deliver me, O Jesus.*
From the desire of being consulted, *deliver me, O Jesus.*

From the desire of being approved, *deliver me, O Jesus.*
From the fear of being humiliated, *deliver me, O Jesus.*
From the fear of being despised, *deliver me, O Jesus.*
From the fear of suffering rebukes, *deliver me, O Jesus.*
From the fear of being belittled, *deliver me, O Jesus.*
From the fear of being forgotten, *deliver me, O Jesus.*
From the fear of being ridiculed, *deliver me, O Jesus.*
From the fear of being wronged, *deliver me, O Jesus.*
From the fear of being suspected, *deliver me, O Jesus.*
That others may be loved more than I, *O Jesus,*
    grant me the grace to desire it.
That others may be esteemed more than I, *O Jesus,*
    grant me the grace to desire it.
That in the opinion of the world, others may increase,
    and I may decrease, *O Jesus, grant me the grace to desire it.*
That others may be chosen, and I set aside,
    O Jesus, grant me the grace to desire it.
That others may be praised and I unnoticed,
    O Jesus, grant me the grace to desire it.
That others may be preferred to me in everything,
    O Jesus, grant me the grace to desire it.
That others become holier than I,
    provided that I may become as holy as I should,
    O Jesus, grant me the grace to desire it.

CARDINAL MERRY DEL VAL

TO ACCEPT SUFFERING

O my Lord, Jesus Christ, I believe that nothing great is done without suffering, and all things are possible by means of it. I believe, O my God, that poverty is better than riches, pain better than pleasure, obscurity and contempt better than good repute, and ignominy and reproach better than honor.

My dear Lord, though I am so very weak that I am not fit to ask for suffering as a gift, and have not the strength to endure it, at least I would ask of you the grace to meet suffering well, when you in your wisdom lay it upon me. Amen.

JOHN CARDINAL NEWMAN

FOR JOY

O You who are the sun of righteousness and the light eternal, giving gladness to all things, shine both on us now and forever, that we may be glad and cheerful for you, for your name's sake. Amen.

ANCIENT PRAYER

FOR PEACE

Lead me from death to life,
From falsehood to truth.
Lead me from despair to hope,
From fear to trust.
Lead me from hate to love,
From war to peace.
Let peace fill our hearts,
Our world, our universe.
Let us dream together,
pray together,
work together,
to build one world
of peace and justice for all.

MOTHER TERESA OF CALCUTTA

FOR RECONCILIATION

May I be no one's enemy, and may I be the friend
of that which is eternal and abides.

May I never quarrel with those nearest me; and,

    if I do, may I be reconciled quickly.

May I love, seek, and attain only that which is good.

May I wish for the happiness of all and envy no one.

May I never rejoice in the ill-fortune of one who has wronged me.

May I win no victory that harms either me or my opponent.

May I reconcile friends who are angry with one another.

May I, to the extent of my power,

    give all needed help to my friends and all who are in want.

May I never fail a friend who is in danger.

May I respect myself. Amen.

EUSEBIUS OF CAESAREA

FOR PATIENCE

Lord Jesus, you are the model of patience and its reward. Urge me to patience and grant it to me. Your own example strengthens me in every conflict, and the reward of my endurance is the gift of your presence. Either way, you win me to yourself. Beckon me on, then; gladly let me follow, and yet even more gladly let me take joy in your presence. For if you are so good to those who seek, what will you not be to those who find? Amen.

SAINT BERNARD OF CLAIRVAUX

FOR SELF-KNOWLEDGE

Lord Jesus, let me know myself; let me know you, and desire nothing else but you. Let me love myself only if I love you, and do all things for your sake.

Let me humble myself and exalt you, and think of nothing else but you. Let me die to myself and live in you, and take whatever happens as coming from you.

Let me forsake myself and walk after you, and ever desire to follow you. Let me flee from myself and turn to you, so that I may merit being defended by you. Let me fear for myself, let me fear for you. And let me be among those who are chosen by you.

Let me distrust myself and trust in you, and ever obey for the love of you. Let me cling to nothing but you, and ever be poor because of you. Look upon me that I may love you, call me, that I may see you, and forever possess you, for all eternity. Amen.

SAINT AUGUSTINE

2. Prayers for Particular Groups

PRAYER FOR MISSIONARIES

Lord Jesus Christ, watch over your missionaries—priests, religious, and lay people—who leave everything to give testimony to your Word and your love.

In difficult moments sustain their energies, comfort their hearts, and crown their work with spiritual achievements.

Let the adorable image of you crucified on the Cross, which accompanies them throughout life, speak to them of heroism, generosity, love, and peace. Amen.

POPE JOHN XXIII

PRAYER FOR PERSECUTED CHRISTIANS

Father, in your mysterious providence, your Church must share in the sufferings of Christ your Son. Give the spirit of patience and love to those who are persecuted for their faith in you that they may always be true and faithful witnesses to your promise of eternal life. Amen.

PRAYER FOR REFUGEES

Lord, no one is a stranger to you and no one is ever far from your loving care. In your kindness watch over refugees and others exiled from their homes, those separated from their loved ones, young people who are lost, and those who have left or run away from home. Bring them back safely to the place where they long to be and help us always to show your kindness to strangers and to those in need. Amen.

PRAYER FOR PRISONERS

Father of mercy, the secrets of all hearts are known to you alone. You know who is just and you forgive the unjust. Hear our prayers for those in prison. Give them patience and hope in their sufferings, and bring them home again soon. Amen.

PRAYER FOR WORKERS

Lord Jesus, carpenter of Nazareth, you were once a worker. Give to me and all the workers of the world the gift of working as you did so that everything we do is for the benefit of our coworkers and the greater glory of God.

May your kingdom come into our workplaces, as well as to our communities and our homes. Give us this day our daily bread; may we receive it graciously and in justice. To we who work and who are heavily burdened, send the refreshment of your love. Show us your way to work, and when it is done may we, with all our fellow workers, rest in peace. Amen.

FOR LEARNERS, ESPECIALLY THOSE WHO ARE STUDYING THE FAITH

Give all who learn, O Lord, a mind that grasps what is taught. Help them to want knowledge so as to know you better and become fully developed human beings filled with your love.

Send your Holy Spirit to help all students see clearly, to judge wisely, to love what is true, to direct their minds to all that is good and noble on earth and in heaven. Amen.

Prayer Services for Groups and Families

1. Advent Prayer Service

Advent is a time of preparation when we repent and wait in hope for the coming of Christ. It is also a time of prayerful waiting for the growth of Christ in our lives.

OPENING HYMN

"O Come, O Come, Emmanuel"

INVITATION TO PRAY

Leader: We are called together as members of one family in the Lord. With this in mind, we make our prayer.

PSALM

Psalm 80 (79) refers to the years of trial during which God seemed to have forgotten the people of Israel, but he brings them and us back and converts us. He does not abandon his people.

Leader: Lord, bring us back and convert us.
    Let your face shine on us.
All: Restore us, O God of hosts; make your face shine upon us,
    that we may be saved.
Leader: O Lord of hosts, how long will your anger burn
    against the prayers of your people?
All: Restore us, O God of hosts; make your face shine upon us,
    that we may be saved.
Leader: You had a vine you brought from Egypt.
    You drove nations out, to plant it in their land.
All: Turn again, O Lord of hosts, look down from heaven and see;
    care for this vine, and protect the stock your hand has planted.
Leader: Then we will never turn away from you;
    give us life, and we will call on your name.

All: Restore us, O Lord, God of hosts; make your face shine on us, that we may be saved.

READING

Leader: Isaiah 2:3–4: Come, let us go to the mountain of the Lord, to the house of the God of Jacob, that he may teach us his ways and we may walk in his paths. For the teaching comes from Zion, and from Jerusalem the word of Yahweh. He will rule over the nations and settle disputes for many peoples. They will beat their swords into plowshares and their spears into pruning hooks. Nation will not raise sword against nation; they will train for war no more.
All: Come, let us walk in the light of the Lord!

Silent Prayer or Group Sharing

RESPONSES

All: O Lord, make us see your mercy and your love.
Leader: Grant us your light and your salvation.
All: O Lord, make us see your mercy and your love.
Leader: Glory to the Father, and to the Son, and to the Holy Spirit.
All: O Lord, make us see your mercy and your love.

INTERCESSIONS

Leader: O Wisdom, breath of the Most High!
   You reign over all creation. Come and teach us.
All: Lord Jesus, come and save us.
Leader: O Lord, head of the house of Israel. You appeared to Moses in the burning bush and gave him the law on Mount Sinai.
All: Lord Jesus, come and ransom us.
Leader: O Rod of Jesse, you who stand as a sign to all the nations and before whom all kings are silent, come without delay.
All: Lord Jesus, come and save us.

Leader: O Key of David, what you open no one can shut,
    come, open our prison doors and set us free.
All: Lord Jesus, come and ransom us.
Leader: O Radiant Dawn and Source of All Eternal Light,
    come and give light to those who live in darkness.
All: Lord Jesus, come and help us see.
Leader: Come, Desire and King of Nations, come and give us peace.
All: Come, Lord Jesus, come soon.

ADVENT PRAYER

God of hope and promise, as we spend this Advent season in anticipation and hope of your arrival, we ask that your soothing presence be with us. Too often the expectations of our commercialized culture and our family obligations make us feel overextended and anxious. Help us to center on our journey toward Bethlehem. Give us calm moments in which to contemplate the purpose of this time of waiting. May your presence be part of all our preparations and planning. Give us ears to hear the alleluias of the angels. Lead us toward the manger. Guide us with your star to a place of joy and repose. Amen.

CLOSING

Leader: Holy, Holy, Holy Lord.
All: Almighty Ruler of all the world.
Leader: He was, he is, and he will come.
All: Yes, he is near.
Leader: May almighty God have mercy on us,
    forgive us our sins, and bring us to life everlasting.
All: Amen.
Leader: Let us go in the peace of the Lord.
All: Thanks be to God.

2. Thanksgiving Prayer Service

OPENING HYMN

"Now Thank We All Our God"

INVITATION TO PRAYER

Leader: Let us gather to thank the Lord for the richness of his blessings, for all the favors he has bestowed on us in the past year, and ask, through the Holy Spirit, that there will be enough for all to share.

PSALM

Leader: O Lord, our Lord, how great is your name throughout the earth!
All: And your glory in the heavens above.
Leader: When I observe the heavens, the work of your hands,
the moon and the stars you set in their place—
what is man you should be mindful of him,
a human being that you should care for him?
All: Yet you made him a little lower than the angels;
you have crowned him with glory and honor.
Leader: You made him rule over the works of your hands;
you have put all things under his feet—
sheep and oxen without number and even the beasts of the field,
the birds of the air, the fish of the sea.
All: O Lord, our Lord, how great is your name all over the earth!

READING

Leader: Revelation 15:3–4: Great and marvelous are your works, O Lord God, and Master of the universe. Justice and truth guide your steps, O King of the nations. Lord, who will not give honor and glory to your Name? For you alone are holy. All the nations will come and bow before you, for they have now seen your judgments.

162

A COUNTING OF BLESSINGS

Leader: For flowers that bloom about our feet.

All: Father, we thank you.

Leader: For tender grass so fresh and sweet.

All: Father, we thank you.

Leader: For song of bird and hum of bee,
For all things fair we hear or see.

All: Father, we thank you.

Leader: For blue of stream and blue of sky.

All: Father, we thank you.

Leader: For pleasant shade of branches high.

All: Father, we thank you.

Leader: For fragrant air and cooling breeze,
For beauty of the blooming trees.

All: Father, we thank you.

Leader: For this new morning with its light.

All: Father, we thank you.

Leader: For rest and shelter of the night.

All: Father, we thank you.

Leader: For health and food, for love and friends,
For everything your goodness sends.

All: Father in heaven, we thank you. Amen.

RALPH WALDO EMERSON

SILENT PRAYER OR GROUP SHARING

Leader: Let us each take the time to silently or in words
express thanks for the gifts God has given.

INTERCESSIONS

Leader: Let us remember all those who cannot be with us
at our table today.

All: Bless them, O Lord.

Leader: Let us remember all those who are hungry, poor, or homeless.

All: Bless them, O Lord.

Leader: Let us remember all those who are sick and alone.

All: Bless them, O Lord.

THANKSGIVING PRAYER

Leader: God, our Provider, from you comes every good and perfect gift. Hear our grateful praise to you this day. Join us in our joyful feast. When our celebration is done, remind us of your steadfast love and enduring grace. Continue to bless our lives with your mercy and sustain us with your Holy Spirit. Amen.

CLOSING

Leader: O God, you have given us life and set us in a world
that is earmarked by your glory. You have comforted us
with family and friends and aided us through their hands.

All: Let us give thanks to God for all the blessings of our life.

Leader: O God, you have remembered us
when we have forgotten you,
and forgiven us when we turned back to you.

All: Let us give thanks to God for all the blessings of our life.

Leader: May almighty God have mercy on us,
forgive us our sins, and bring us to life everlasting.

All: Amen.

3. Christmas Prayer Service

OPENING HYMN

"O Come All Ye Faithful"

INVITATION TO PRAY

Leader: God, our Father, we gather here together to celebrate the birth of your Son, Jesus. Your people waited many years for his coming, and they rejoiced on the great day of his birth. Help us to realize the real meaning of Christmas, that it is to be found in giving and loving. We pray that this celebration inspire us to live in love and peace. Let every Christmas gift be a reminder of you. Let your name be spoken joyously in every heart, and may you come to light this place with signs of the good tidings of our salvation. Amen.

PSALM

Psalm 98 (97): This psalm tells us to sing a new song to the Lord, for humanity, in the coming of Christ, God-made-man, has found its way to salvation.

Leader: Sing to the Lord a new song, for he has done wonders;
his right hand, his holy arm, has won victory for him.

All: All you lands, make a joyful noise to the Lord, break into song and sing praise. With trumpet blast and sound of the horn, rejoice before the King, the Lord!

Leader: The Lord has shown his salvation,
revealing his justice to the nations.

All: All you lands, make a joyful noise to the Lord, break into song and sing praise. With trumpet blast and sound of the horn, rejoice before the King, the Lord!

Leader: He has not forgotten his love nor his faithfulness to Israel.
To the farthest ends of the earth all have seen God's saving power.

All: All you lands, make a joyful noise to the Lord, break into song and sing praise. With trumpet blast and sound of the horn, rejoice before the King, the Lord!

Leader: Let rivers clap their hands, hills and mountains sing
with joy before the Lord, for he comes to rule the earth.
He will judge the world with justice and the peoples with fairness.
All: All you lands, make a joyful noise to the Lord, break into song
and sing praise. With trumpet blast and sound of the horn,
rejoice before the King, the Lord!

READING

Leader: Luke 2:6–14: They were in Bethlehem when the time came
for her to have her child, and she gave birth to a son, her firstborn.
She wrapped him in swaddling clothes and laid him in the manger,
because there was no place for them in the living room.

There were shepherds camping in the countryside, taking turns
to watch over their flocks by night. Suddenly an angel of the Lord
appeared to them, with the Glory of the Lord shining around them.

As they were terrified, the angel said to them "Don't be afraid; I
am here to give you good news, great joy for all the people. Today a
Savior has been born to you in David's town; he is the Messiah and
the Lord. Let this be a sign to you; you will find a baby wrapped in
swaddling clothes and lying in a manger."

Suddenly the angel was surrounded by many more angels, praising God and saying, "Glory to God in the highest; peace on earth for
God is blessing humankind."

SILENT PRAYER OR GROUP SHARING

RESPONSES

Leader: Now the prophecies are fulfilled:
the light of the Most High has risen in our world.
All: Your almighty Word leapt down from heaven.
Leader: Midway through the night, in deep silence,
All: Your almighty Word leapt down from heaven.

Leader: For the great love that he bore us,
  God sent his Son in flesh like ours.
All: Your almighty Word leapt down from heaven.
  Holy is his name. Amen.

INTERCESSIONS

Leader: O Jesus, a great star brought news of your birth.
All: Let us ever be open to the light of your spirit.
Leader: O Jesus, you were once a tiny infant
  vulnerable to your enemies.
All: Let us ever remember the strength of your spirit.
Leader: O Jesus, you were born into this world
  in order to lead us into the next one.
All: Let us spread your spirit of love to our families
  and throughout the world. Amen.

CHRISTMAS PRAYER

What can I give Him
Poor as I am;
If I were a shepherd
I would give Him a lamb.
  If I were a wise man,
  I would do my part.
  But what can I give Him?
  I will give my heart.

CHRISTINA ROSSETTI

CLOSING

Glory to you, our Lord Jesus Christ; in you is our beginning. In love you made yourself known as a small child; may the secret of your birth remain always in our hearts. Your light shines forth and dispels the darkness, and your love is ever with us, today and every day, world without end. Amen.

4. Lenten Prayer Service

The season of Lent is a time of spiritual retreat. In communion with Christ, we are invited to forty days of prayer, meditation, and sacrifice in preparation for Easter.

OPENING HYMN

"All Glory, Praise, and Honor"

INVITATION TO PRAY

Leader: We are gathered together as the children of God's promise of salvation to mark the season of Lent and to remember the sufferings of Jesus Christ. This is a season to take up our crosses and to be servants of all. This is a season to watch and wait with Christ, that we may have courage in the hour of our testing. This is a season of pilgrimage as we follow in the footsteps of Jesus Christ. Let us go forward in the glorious promise of a new life in Christ. Amen.

PSALM

Psalm 28 (27) is a call for help to the Lord, our God.

Leader: To you, O Lord, I call. For if you heed me not,
  I shall go down to the pit like the rest.
All: O my Lord, my Rock, do not be deaf to my call!
Leader: Hear my cry for mercy as I call to you for help,
  as I lift up my hands toward your innermost sanctuary.
All: O my Lord, my Rock, do not be deaf to my call!
Leader: Drag me not away with the wicked,
  with those who do evil, who mouth words of peace
  while they sow mischief and confusion.

All: O my Lord, my Rock, do not be deaf to my call!

Leader: The Lord is my strength, my shield.

My heart was sure of him, I have been helped

and my heart exults, with my song I give him thanks.

All: O my Lord, my Rock, do not be deaf to my call!

Leader: Save your people, and bless your inheritance.

Be their shepherd and carry them forever.

All: O my Lord, my Rock, do not be deaf to my call!

READING

Leader: Luke 4:1–12: As he returned from the Jordan, the Spirit led [Jesus] into the desert where he was tempted by the devil for forty days. He did not eat anything during that time, and in the end he was hungry. The devil then said to him, "If you are the Son of God, tell this stone to turn into bread." But Jesus answered, "Scripture says: *People cannot live on bread alone."*

Then the devil took him up to a high place and showed him in a flash all the nations of the world. And he said to Jesus, "I can give you power over all the nations and their wealth will be yours, for power and wealth have been delivered to me and I give them to anyone I choose. All this will be yours provided you worship me." But Jesus replied, "Scripture says: *You shall worship the Lord your God and serve him alone."*

Then the devil took him up to Jerusalem and set him on the highest wall of the Temple; and he said, "If you are the son of God, throw yourself down from here, for it is written: *God will order his angels to take care of you* and again: *They will hold you in their hands, lest you hurt your foot on the stones."* But Jesus replied, "It is written: *You shall not challenge the Lord your God."*

SILENT PRAYER OR GROUP SHARING

RESPONSES

Leader: The angels will bear you in their hands,
and your foot will not stumble on a stone.
All: Worthy is the lamb that was slain;
strength, honor, and praise to Him!
Leader: From the snare of the hunter, he will deliver you.
All: Worthy is the lamb that was slain;
strength, honor, and praise to Him!
Leader: Stretch out your strong hand
to all who are in danger and distress;
sustain us by your Father's word, which nourished you in the desert.
All: Worthy is the lamb that was slain;
strength, honor, and praise to Him!

INTERCESSIONS

Leader: Transform the sorrows of our faults into the joy of pardon,
and in your goodness, hasten the return of Jesus Christ, our Lord.
All: Comfort us, O Lord, and have mercy on us!
Leader: Free us from evil and gather us into the peace
proclaimed by your death on the Cross.
All: Comfort us, O Lord, and have mercy on us!
Leader: Guide in the ways of eternal life
all those whom we have entrusted to you through our prayers.
All: Comfort us, O Lord, and have mercy on us!
Leader: Strengthen in us our vocation
to love and serve you faithfully.
All: Comfort us, O Lord, and have mercy on us!
Leader: Remember how easily we fall;
we are weak by nature, weak by ability,
and the evil in us is cleverly hidden.
All: Comfort us, O Lord, and have mercy on us!

LENTEN PRAYER

Leader: God of all mercy and steadfast love, we do not always live the way you want us to. Forgive us. Help us during this season of Lent to examine how we can be more faithful followers of Jesus Christ, your Son. Guide us in our pilgrimage of discipleship. May our words and actions truly reflect your will for us. In the name of Jesus, our Savior, we pray. Amen.

CLOSING

Leader: O Christ, remember us in your Kingdom.

O Lord, teach us to pray:

All: Our Father, who art in heaven, hallowed be thy name.

Thy kingdom come; thy will be done on earth as it is in heaven.

Give us this day our daily bread; and forgive us our trespasses

as we forgive those who trespass against us;

and lead us not into temptation, but deliver us from evil. Amen.

Leader: May God the Father, and our Lord Jesus Christ,

grant us peace and love.

All: Amen.

5. Easter Prayer Service

Easter is the celebration of the Resurrection of our Lord. The joyful weeks that follow lead up to the celebration of Christ's Ascension. The forty days between Easter and the Ascension are in contrast to the forty days of Lent.

OPENING HYMN

"Jesus Christ Is Risen Today"

INVITATION TO PRAY

Leader: Almighty God, we welcome this feast of Easter, this feast of joy and renewal. Together we proclaim the good news of your eternal love for us. Let us remember that the Word of God was made flesh in this world through Jesus Christ. The Light shone in the shadows of sin. Let us ever reflect the light of the risen Christ in our lives. We are called to spread the good news of this day to all the world. Christ is risen! Alleluia!

PSALM

Psalm 47 (46) declares that the Lord, the king of all nations, comes at the end of time to begin his reign.

Leader: Clap your hands, all you peoples;
　　acclaim God with shouts of joy. For the Lord, the Most High,
　　is to be feared; he is a great king all over the earth.
All: Sing praises to God, sing praises!
　　Sing praises to our King, sing praises!
Leader: He brings peoples under our dominion
　　and puts nations under our feet. He chose our inheritance for us—
　　the pride of Jacob whom he loves!
All: Sing praises to God, sing praises!
　　Sing praises to our King, sing praises!
Leader: God ascends amid joyful shouts, the Lord amid trumpet blasts.
All: Sing praises to God, sing praises!
　　Sing praises to our King, sing praises!
Leader: God is king of all the earth; sing to him a hymn of praise.
　　For God now rules over the nations, God reigns from his holy throne.
All: Sing praises to God, sing praises!
　　Sing praises to our King, sing praises!

READING

Leader: John 20:1–9. Now, on the first day after the sabbath, Mary of Magdala came to the tomb early in the morning, while it was still dark and she saw that the stone blocking the tomb had been moved away. She ran to Peter and the other disciple whom Jesus loved. And she said to them, "They have taken the Lord out of the tomb and we don't know where they have laid him."

Peter then set out with the other disciple to go to the tomb. They ran together but the other disciple outran Peter and reached the tomb first. He bent down and saw the linen cloths lying flat, but he did not enter.

Then Simon Peter came following him and entered the tomb; he, too, saw the linen cloths lying flat. The napkin, which had been around his head was not lying flat like the other linen cloths but lay rolled up in its place. Then the other disciple who had reached the tomb first also went in; he saw and believed. Scripture clearly said that he must rise from the dead, but they had not yet understood that.

SILENT PRAYER OR GROUP SHARING

RESPONSES

Leader: Father, your Son and faithful servant brought healing to those
who were sick, words of comfort to those who were in need.
And they killed him, hanging him on a tree.

All: Jesus Christ has risen from the dead and dies now no more.
Alleluia.

Leader: Teach us now to walk the path he walked before us,
speaking peace when people cry out in pain, bringing healing
to the wounds that scar our world, and dying also with him.

All: Jesus Christ has risen from the dead and dies now no more.
Alleluia.

Leader: But you raised him up to life, and so promise
to raise us up with him. This is the message you have sent to us;
this is the message we must preach.

All: Jesus Christ has risen from the dead and dies now no more.
Alleluia.

Leader: All glory be to you, Father, now and forever.

All: Jesus Christ has risen from the dead and dies now no more. Alleluia.

INTERCESSIONS

Leader: O Good Shepherd, who was raised to life,
make us ever ready to do your will in all things.

All: Hear us, Lord of Glory.

Leader: O Christ, in your Resurrection,
you have burst the gates of the dwelling of the dead.
You have destroyed sin and death.
By your victory, we ask you: keep us victorious over sin.

All: Hear us, Lord of Glory.

Leader: O Lord, Jesus Christ, in your Resurrection
you have rendered death powerless.
You have given us new life. By your victory,
we ask you to direct our lives as your new creation.

All: Hear us, Lord of Glory.

Leader: O Paschal Victim, in your Resurrection,
you gladdened your disciples. By your victory we ask you:
give us joy in your service.

All: Hear us, Lord of Glory.

EASTER PRAYER

Leader: Lord God, your generous faithfulness puts us to shame. You have never given up on us, even though our history is one of unfaithfulness and discouragement. You have raised the dead to life in your Son, and are raising us to new life each time we set aside ourselves to serve someone else. Having shared in the new life of Jesus, we praise you and bless you for your mercy. In his name we pray forever and ever. Amen.

CLOSING

Leader: Blessings and courage to you who have come
in acceptance of the Lord's invitation to follow him.
May the strength and peace of the risen Christ be with you.
All: Amen! Alleluia!

6. Pentecost Prayer Service

Pentecost celebrates the beginning of the Church, marking the day when the followers of Jesus were filled with the Holy Spirit. Pentecost also reminds us that the Holy Spirit empowers all of us to proclaim the saving power of Christ.

OPENING HYMN

"Come, Holy Spirit, Creator Blest"

INVITATION TO PRAYER

As the leader extends an invitation to pray, various members of the assembly or family light twelve candles.

Leader: Together we gather to celebrate Pentecost, remembering the beginnings of the Church and celebrating the presence of the Holy Spirit among us. We light three candles to remind us this day of our past, present, and future as people of God. We light three candles to remind us of God's presence among us as God the Father, God the Son, and God the Holy Spirit. We light three candles to signify the presence of the Holy Spirit on our lips, in our hearts, and in our understanding. We light three candles to remind us of the three virtues of faith, hope, and love. Holy Spirit of flame and fire, remain with us today and always. As we leave this gathering today, send us forth with your blessing to be reactivated disciples of your Word. Amen.

PSALM

Psalm 104 (103) is a hymn of praise for the Creator of the universe.

Leader: Bless the Lord, my soul! Clothed in majesty and splendor;
O Lord, my God, how great you are!

All: When you send forth your spirit, they are created, and the face
of the earth is renewed. May the glory of the Lord endure forever.

Leader: You are wrapped in light as with a garment;
you stretch out the heavens like a tent,
you build your upper rooms above the waters.

All: When you send forth your spirit, they are created, and the face
of the earth is renewed. May the glory of the Lord endure forever.

Leader: You make the clouds your chariot
and ride on the wings of the wind;
you make the winds your messengers,
and fire and flame your ministers.

All: When you send forth your spirit, they are created, and the face
of the earth is renewed. May the glory of the Lord endure forever.

Leader: You set the earth on its foundations,
and never will it be shaken.
You covered it with ocean like a garment,
and waters spread over the mountains.

All: When you send forth your spirit, they are created, and the face
of the earth is renewed. May the glory of the Lord endure forever.

Leader: You made the moon to mark the seasons,
and the sun that knows when to set;
when you bring the darkness of the night,
all the beasts of the forest begin to prowl: the young lions
roaring for their prey claiming their food from God.

All: When you send forth your spirit, they are created, and the face
of the earth is renewed. May the glory of the Lord endure forever.

Leader: They all look to you for their food in due time.

> You give it to them, and they gather it up; you open your hand, they are filled with good things.

All: When you send forth your spirit, they are created, and the face of the earth is renewed. May the glory of the Lord endure forever.

Leader: He looks on the earth, and it quakes;

> he touches the mountain, and it smokes.
>
> I will sing to the Lord all my life;
>
> I will sing praise to God while I live.

All: When you send forth your spirit, they are created, and the face of the earth is renewed. May the glory of the Lord endure forever.

READING

Leader: Acts 2:1–4: When the day of Pentecost came, they were all together in one place. And suddenly out of the sky came a sound like a strong rushing wind and it filled the whole house where they were sitting. There appeared tongues as if of fire which parted and came to rest upon each one of them. All were filled with Holy Spirit and began to speak other languages, as the Spirit enabled them to speak.

RESPONSES

Leader: In the beginning you breathed the breath of life into Adam,

> now you send the Holy Spirit into your Church
>
> to bring new life to the whole world.

All: Come, Holy Spirit, and make the whole world new.

Leader: By the light of your Spirit, enlighten the world

> and send your mighty wind to break down the barriers
>
> that separate us from our brothers and sisters.

All: Come, Holy Spirit, and make the whole world new.

Leader: Water flowed from the side of Christ

> as the fountain of your spirit.

May it flow over all the earth, bringing forth goodness and love.
All: Come, Holy Spirit, and make the whole world new.
Leader: Come, Holy Spirit.
All: In the name of the Father and the Son. Amen.

INTERCESSIONS

Leader: The Holy Spirit comes to assist us in our weakness, alleluia.
All: Strengthen us, O Holy Spirit!
Leader: Living God!

Come and make us temples of your Holy Spirit.

Baptize us with fire

that we may stand always as a pillar of your love.
All: Strengthen us, O Holy Spirit!
Leader: Give to us all the fruits of the Holy Spirit,

love, peace, joy, patience, kindness, faithfulness.
All: Strengthen us, O Holy Spirit!
Leader: Send the Comforter to all who are passing through difficulties

or who are victims of human evil.
All: Strengthen us, O Holy Spirit!
Leader: Preserve from hatred and war every nation, every people,

and create a new community among them

by the power of your wisdom.
All: Strengthen us, O Holy Spirit!
Leader: Holy Spirit, Giver of Life, Spirit of counsel and might,

of understanding and of prayer:
All: Strengthen us, O Holy Spirit!

PENTECOST PRAYER

Leader: God of many gifts, today we celebrate the power and presence of your Holy Spirit among all humanity. Through Jesus Christ we are united as one body. May your visions of truth and dreams of peace, proclaimed by your prophets, be made a reality in our midst.

Come, Holy Spirit, bless those gathered here. Celebrate this day of renewal and hope with us. Breathe into us new life. Send us forth to be your witnesses to the ends of the earth. Amen.

CLOSING

Leader: A new day has dawned. God's gift of life is renewed in us.
All: Praise God for the new spirit in our midst!
Leader: Be still and know that the Spirit has come.
All: Come, rejoice, and let the Spirit in.
Leader: Let us listen and respond to the Holy Spirit
who meets us in new ways today and every day.
All: Fill us with faith, and enable us to grow
toward a deeper understanding of your will for us,
through the power of the Holy Spirit. Amen.

7. A Prayer Service for Yom HaShoah: Holocaust Remembrance Day

The Days of Remembrance (Yom HaShoah) are observed each year on the 27th of Nisan on the Jewish calendar. This date falls on the fifth day following the eighth day of Passover. Official proclamations are issued and ceremonies conducted by the president of the United States, the governors of all fifty states, the mayors of all major American cities, and military, government, and community groups, universities and schools, and of course, in synagogues and churches. Days of Remembrance provide Jews and Christians an opportunity to come together and engage in healing. It is a time for members of the community to unite in reflection, commemoration, and bearing witness. The aim of Days of Remembrance is to recollect the human tragedy visited upon the Jewish people, to seek reconciliation, and to renew commitment to life.

OPENING HYMN

"O God, Our Help in Ages Past" (Text: Psalm 98, adapted by Isaac Watts [d. 1748], Music: William Croft [d. 1727]); or "Amazing Grace" (Text: John Newton [d. 1807], Music: *Virginia Harmony*, 1831); or "Be Not Afraid" (Text: Isaiah 43, Luke 6, Music: Bob Dufford, SJ).

INVITATION TO PRAY

Leader: O God, as we gather today in prayer we remember the evils in the past: the innocents enslaved and tortured and murdered. We ask for wisdom that we might never forget and yet not lose hope. We ask for wisdom that we may face the evil, and vow that those who died will not have suffered in vain. And so we pray: For those who were given death, let us choose life. For those who found the courage to stand against evil, let us promise to carry on their struggles. Let us pray that we may learn from hate that we must love, and that we may learn from evil that we must live for good. Amen.

PSALM

Psalm 22 (21) is a lament of the persecuted. As this psalm is recited, a member of the group may light six candles in remembrance of the six million Jews killed in the Holocaust.

All: My God, my God, why have you forsaken me?

Why are you so far from me, from the sound of my groaning?

Leader: My God, I call by day, but you never answer;

by night and I find no rest.

All: Yet you are enthroned the Holy One, the praise of Israel.

In you our fathers trusted, and you delivered them.

They cried to you and they were saved;

they trusted in you and were not overcome.

READING

Leader: Mt 25:42–45: For I was hungry and you did not give me anything to eat, I was thirsty and you gave me nothing to drink; I was a stranger and you did not welcome me into your house; I was naked and you did not clothe me; I was sick and in prison and you did not visit me.

They, too, will ask: "Lord, when did we see you hungry, thirsty, naked or a stranger, sick or in prison, and did not help you?" The King will answer them: "Truly, I say to you; whatever you did not do for one of the least of these, you did not do for me."

READING

Pope John Paul II, who knew well of Nazi inhumanity, prayed this prayer during his pilgrimage to Auschwitz in 1979:

Leader: I kneel before all the inscriptions that come one after another bearing the memory of the victims of Auschwitz....In particular I pause with you, dear participants in this encounter, before the inscription in Hebrew. This inscription awakens the memory of the people whose sons and daughters were intended for total extermination. This people draws its origins from Abraham, our father in faith as was expressed by Paul of Tarsus. The very people who received from God the commandment "thou shalt not kill" itself experiences in a special measure what is meant by killing. It is not permissible for anyone to pass by this inscription with indifference.

SILENT PRAYER OR GROUP SHARING

RESPONSES

The Reverend Martin Niemoeller, a pastor in the German Confessing Church, spent seven years in a concentration camp. He wrote the following words:

Leader: First they came for the communists, and I did not speak out—
All: Because I was not a communist.
Leader: Then they came for the socialists, and I did not speak out—
All: Because I was not a socialist.
Leader: Then they came for the trade unionists, and I did not speak out—
All: Because I was not a trade unionist.
Leader: Then they came for the Jews, and I did not speak out—
All: Because I was not a Jew.
Leader: Then they came for me—
All: And there was no one left to speak out for me.

INTERCESSIONS

Leader: For our forgetting of those faces
    who never find a secure resting place,
All: Forgive us, O God.
Leader: For our indifference to those whose bodies are broken
    and whose minds are weak,
    and our callousness to those
    who have been orphaned and widowed,
    deserted and driven from their homes,
All: Forgive us, O God.
Leader: For our disdain of others who worship or believe differently,
All: Forgive us, O God.
Leader: For our feeling of comfort
    in that we are no longer bothered by the misery of others,
All: Forgive us, O God.
Leader: For our sin of wounding people
    with unkind words or insulting characterizations,
All: Forgive us, O God.
Leader: For our willingness to close our hearts and our homes
    to those of other races,

All: Forgive us, O God.

Leader: For the sins we have committed

by not seeing God's image in every human being,

All: For all these sins, O merciful God,

forgive us, pardon us, grant us atonement. Amen.

YOM HASHOAH PRAYER

Leader: Compassionate God, grant perfect peace in your glorious presence to all the souls of our brethren, men, women, and children, who were slaughtered and burned. May their memories endure in our lives. May their souls be thus bound up in the bond of life. May they rest in peace. And let us say: Amen.

CLOSING

A kaddish is a prayer of mourning said every day in the synagogue. Here are the words:

May your glory, O King of Kings, be exalted.

O You who shall renew the world

and let the defunct rise again.

Your rule, Adonai, shall be proclaimed by us,

the children of Israel, today, tomorrow, always.

Let us say: Amen

May it be loved, may it be cherished.

Amen.

Prayers for the Sick, Dying, and the Deceased

1. Prayers for the Sick

TO CHRIST, OUR HEALER

The physician our Lord and Savior is all powerful.
He restores those who worship and hope in him.
He heals not by the skill of science but by his word.
Though he dwells in heaven, he is present everywhere.
All praise to him. Amen.

AN EARLY CHRISTIAN MARTYR

PRAYER FOR HEALING

Jesus, you are my deliverer, the true physician who comes all the way from heaven to visit the sick. I put myself into your hands. Help me to resolve to put all my trust in you alone and to patiently undergo any treatment. If you will not heal me, my Savior, my case is beyond hope. But if I am to be healed, it is you, Lord, who will heal me. You alone uproot the sickness and give me lasting health. You are my salvation and life, my comfort and glory, my hope in this world and my crown in the world to come. Amen.

PRAYER TO SAINT PEREGRINE FOR REMISSION OF CANCER

Saint Peregrine, you left a life of comfort to dedicate yourself to the salvation of all peoples. You endured the most painful sufferings with such patience that you were healed miraculously. With a touch of the divine hand, your incurable leg wound disappeared.

Obtain for us, Dear Saint, the grace of resignation to our present suffering with cancer. Enkindle in our hearts perfect resignation to what God has in store for us. But, if it is in God's plan, deliver us, through your intercession with our crucified Lord and our sorrowful Mother, from this sickness that is afflicting our bodies. If this is not possible, enable us to merit everlasting glory in paradise. Amen.

PRAYER TO SAINT GERARD MAJELLA FOR A MOTHER AT RISK

O my God and Savior who, through the empowerment of the Holy Spirit, created a worthy home in the womb of the Blessed Virgin Mary for your Son, listen to my prayer. I ask you through the intercession of Saint Gerard Majella, your faithful servant, to protect me (her) from the dangers of motherhood and keep from all evil the baby you have entrusted to me (her), so that, by your saving grace, this child may receive holy baptism. Grant also that after living a life of joy in your service on this earth, both mother and child may attain everlasting happiness in heaven. Amen.

DAILY PRAYER DURING SICKNESS

Almighty God, I receive this sickness as coming from your hand. It is your will that it should come to me, and I accept it from your fatherly hand. I offer this sickness in honor of your Holy Name and for the good of my soul. I am your creature and I am pleased to suffer what you will for as long as you please and in whatever manner you please, for I have offended you with my lack of gratitude and the severity of my sins.

Truly I deserve your rebuke but look upon my weakness and deal with me not according to my sins but according to your compassion and tender mercy. Give me the strength to bear with patience all the pains, discomforts, anxieties, and trials of my sickness. If it is your will that this sickness is my last, I ask of you to direct me by your grace so that I may receive those sacraments which you have instituted for the good of my soul, to prepare it for its passage into eternity. I put my whole trust in you, dear Lord, and love you above all things. Through the merits of your passion and death, may I be admitted into the company of the blessed, there to reside with you forever and ever. Amen.

PRAYER FOR THE SICK

Let us ask the Lord of all health and salvation on behalf of our brothers and sisters who are suffering from bodily illnesses that he alone who is the Dear Physician will help them all.

O God, who bids our lives to run fast or slow, accept the prayers of your servants who in their sickness implore your pity. Save them and change their fear and apprehension to joy.

We call on you, Lord, who has formed our bodies and souls and who governs, guides, and saves all of humankind, may our prayers move you to relent and heal all who are sick, remove their suffering from them, raise up those who must convalesce in bed, so that they may glorify your Holy Name, now and forever. Amen.

PRAYER BEFORE AN OPERATION

O Father of all life, I come to you for help. I commit myself to you with perfect trust as I prepare to undergo this surgery. Protect me in this hour of pain. Guide the hands of your servants who will perform and assist at this procedure, and give them success so that the outcome of their endeavors will be a sign of your goodness. Finally grant that I may bear any suffering with cheerfulness and be the means of helping others in their time of trial. Amen.

PRAYER BEFORE CHEMOTHERAPY, RADIATION, OR OTHER PAINFUL PROCEDURE

O my Savior, who underwent such suffering for me on the Cross with consciousness and firmness, help me as I face this terrible trial and the physical pain associated with it. Enable me to bear this procedure with some measure of your calmness. May the radiation that enters my body be as your light so that it is you, O Lord, who heals me. May the chemicals that flow into my bloodstream be as your saving grace so that it is you, O Lord, who cures my illness. May the

189

instruments associated with this medical procedure be as your saving hands so that it is you, O Lord, who grants me lasting health. If I suffer, let me suffer along with you, so that these sufferings may be a sign of repentance for my sins. Amen.

PRAYER DURING SUFFERING

Lord Jesus Christ, accept my sufferings and unite them to yours on the Cross. Sanctify this sickness and give me the grace to welcome it. Support me in my pain and weakness and comfort me in my affliction, and let me rest my weariness and pain in your loving heart. Relieve me and refresh me so that I may bear this suffering for your sake.

You who comforted the martyrs in their torture and gave them courage, renew your comfort in me. Defend me against all temptations and keep the enemy from taking advantage of me in this illness. Above all, give me strength to bear whatever you have chosen for me. Amen.

THANKSGIVING FOR RECOVERY

Glory to you, heavenly Father, for the sickness you have sent me. My illness has humbled me and reminded me of your laws. Let me keep your word always.

Glory to you, O Lord, for delivering me from the terrors of pain and restoring me to health. Your hear me in my trouble, and so I will live to declare the praises of my God.

Glory to you, O Lord God, for the lengthening of my life on this earth. Give me the grace to spend this life in your service and to perform all my resolutions with willing obedience.

When you finally decide that my time has come, let me die at peace with you, at peace with the world, and at peace with myself.

The blessing of God Almighty, the Father, the Son, and the Holy Spirit, descend on me and all belonging to me, and be with me in my going out and my coming in, now and forever. Amen.

2. Prayers for the Dying

TERESA OF ÁVILA'S LAST PRAYER

My Lord, it is time to move on.
Well, then, may your will be done.
O my Lord and my Spouse,
The house that I have longed for has come.
It is time for us to meet one another. Amen.

TERESA OF ÁVILA

A CALL TO THE KINGDOM

It has pleased you, Lord, to keep me until this time.
I thought, for a while, that you had rejected me as being
A stone not fit for your heavenly building;
But now that you call me to take my place in it,
I am ready to suffer that I may have a part
In your kingdom with all of your saints. Amen.

MARTYR FROM DALMATIA

PRAYER FOR A PERSON ON HIS OR HER DEATHBED

Merciful God, who has given humankind saving remedies and the gifts of everlasting life, look mercifully on this person who is grievously sick and comfort the soul you have created. Let this person be found worthy at the hour of death to be presented by your holy angels, free from all stain of sin, to you, the maker of all creatures. Amen.

PRAYER FOR A GOOD DEATH

Good Lord, give me the grace so as to spend my life, that when the day of my death shall come, though I feel pain in my body, I may feel comfort in my soul; and with the faithful hope of your mercy, with all the love that is due to you, and with charity toward the world, I may, through your grace, depart into your everlasting glory. Amen.

SAINT THOMAS MORE

THE FLOWERS OF DEATH

This death, which seems so terrible,
   is little enough price to pay for eternal life.
Savior, receive a branch of the tree;
   it will decay, but it will flower again
   and be clothed in glory.
The vine dies in winter, yet revives in spring.
Shall not this life which is cut down rise again?
My heart rejoices in the Lord
   and my soul has exulted in my salvation.
Amen.

A PERSIAN MARTYR

PRAYER FOR THOSE IN THEIR FINAL AGONY

O most merciful Jesus, lover of souls, I pray that you, by the agony endured by your most Sacred Heart, and by the sorrows of your Immaculate Mother, with your own blood, cleanse the sinners of the whole world who are now in their final agony and who are to die this day. Heart of Jesus, have pity on the dying. Amen.

PRAYER AT DEATH'S LAST MOMENT

Into your hands, O Lord, I resign my spirit.
Lord Jesus Christ, receive my spirit.
Holy Mary, pray for me.
Mary, mother of grace, mother of mercy,
   guard me from the enemy, and receive me at the hour of death.
Saint Joseph, pray for me.

Saint Joseph, with your blessed virgin-wife,
    open for me the bosom of divine mercy.
Jesus, Mary, Joseph, I give you my heart and my soul.
Jesus, Mary, Joseph, stand by me in my last agony.
Jesus, Mary, Joseph, may I sleep and rest in peace with you.
Amen.

PRAYER TO COMMEND THE SOUL AT THE MOMENT OF DEATH

I commend you, my dear brother (or sister),
    to almighty God and entrust you to your Creator.
May you return to him who formed you from the dust of the earth.
May holy Mary, the angels, and all the saints come to meet you
    as you go forth from this life.
May Christ, who was crucified for you,
    bring you freedom and peace.
May Christ, who died for you,
    admit you into his garden of paradise.
May Christ, the true Shepherd, acknowledge you as one of his flock.
May he forgive you all your sins and set you
    among those he has chosen.
May you see your Redeemer face to face and enjoy the vision of God
    forever and ever.
Amen.

3. Prayers for the Deceased

INVOCATION FOR THE DEAD

Eternal rest grant unto them, O Lord; and let perpetual light shine
upon them. May they rest in peace.
Merciful Lord Jesus, grant them everlasting rest.
Amen.

ADDRESS TO THE DEAD

When you are dead and the Lord has said to you, "Here am I, my child," I will come to your grave. I will bring whatever is on my soul, whatever may have happened to me, and I will come to you as when you were alive and, kneeling on the ground, cast all my bitterness on your grave. I will tell you everything and you will listen to me, and all the bitterness will fly away from me. And as you spoke to me when I was alive, you will do so now. For you are living, and you shall be forever. Amen.

ADAPTED FROM THE WORDS OF SAINT SERAPHIM

PRAYER FOR A DEPARTED LOVED ONE

Almighty God, my soul is full of agony. You have taken one I loved from my eyes and I have no one to help me. My heart is desolate. Please comfort me, for I am in great trouble.

Teach me, O God, in this hour of sorrow, in this great bereavement, on this most bitter day, to have patience and Christian resignation. Teach me to follow your will with meekness as well as strength. You know my sorrows and my tears. Look upon me and give me help. Enable me to bear the weight of this trial, for I am unable to bear it alone. Pity me, Good Lord; pity me, Gracious Father; for Christ's sake turn your face toward me and mercifully accept my prayer. Amen.

FOR THOSE WE ARE BOUND TO PRAY FOR

Grant, we ask of you, O Lord our God, that the souls of your sons and daughters, whose memory we should keep with special reverence, and for whom we are bound to pray, and for the souls of all parents, our benefactors, our relations and family members, and all the rest of the faithful, may rest in the safe heart of your saints; and hereafter in the resurrection from the dead, may they please you in life everlasting. Amen.

PRAYER FOR THE SOULS IN PURGATORY

Most merciful Jesus, I offer you the virtues and merits of your holy life and your passion, and also the merits of your Mother, the Blessed Virgin Mary and of all the saints. I offer them to your divine Father for all the souls in purgatory.

Most faithful Jesus, draw from your wounds and your heart those blessings that will give eternal rest to the souls of the departed. Most merciful Jesus, through your compassionate heart, grant eternal rest to each and all of them.

I pray to you, through the kindness of your heart, to take pity on the souls detained in purgatory. Remember, O Jesus, the mercies you have shown toward us; remember your pains, the wounds you have received, the blood you have shed, and finally the very bitter death you have accepted for us. In consideration of all these things, I ask you to pour out on the souls in purgatory the virtues, fruits, and merits of your sufferings and passion, in order that each soul may be entirely released, or at least greatly relieved.

O Jesus, remember that these are your friends, your children, your elect, whom you have redeemed. Let your justice be satisfied with the great punishment they have endured already. For your own sake, O Lord, show mercy and remit the rest of their sufferings. Amen.

PRAYER FOR THE DEAD

O God who has defeated death and granted the gift of life to the world, give to your departed sons and daughters repose and security in which pain and grief are forgotten. As you are a good and loving God, pardon every one of their sins of thought, word, and deed.

O Savior who has purchased mortals with your own blood and redeemed them by your death, grant to us by your Resurrection life everlasting. Give rest, Lord, to all the faithful departed, whether in desert lands or in cities, on the sea or on the shore; to those of ry age and race. Make them all worthy of your heavenly kingdom. Amen.

ANTIPHON FOR THE DEAD

May the angels lead you into paradise,
May the martyrs receive you at your coming
And bring you into the holy city, into Jerusalem.
May a choir of angels welcome you;
And there, where Lazarus is poor no longer,
May you have eternal rest.

WELCOME INTO HEAVEN

Receive, Lord, the souls of your servants who come home to you. Clothe them with a heavenly garment and wash them in the holy fountain of everlasting life, so that they may be glad with the glad, wise with the wise.

Let them take their seats among the crowned martyrs, move among the patriarchs and prophets, and follow Christ in the company of the apostles.

Let them contemplate the splendor of God among the angels and archangels; let them rejoice within the gleaming walks of paradise; let them have knowledge of the divine mysteries and find the brightness of God among the cherubim and seraphim.

Let them wash their robes together with those who wash their garments in the fountain of lights; and knocking, find the gates of heavenly Jerusalem open to them. Let them see God face to face in that company, and savor the ineffable strains of celestial music. Amen.

SECTION ELEVEN

Prayers to the
Holy Angels and the Saints

1. Prayers to Saint Joseph

PRAYER OF DEDICATION TO SAINT JOSEPH

O glorious Saint Joseph, chosen by God to be the foster father of Jesus, the spouse of Mary ever virgin, and the head of the Holy Family, and then appointed as the heavenly patron and defender of the Church, I ask for your powerful intercession for all members of the Church, those who lead and those who follow, those who labor for souls in faraway lands and those who struggle to lead a holy life within their own homes.

Be pleased, dear Saint Joseph, to accept this dedication of myself which I now make to you. I dedicate myself to you as my father and my guide in the way of salvation. Obtain for me purity of heart and an unshakable devotion to the interior life. Grant that, following your example, I may point all my actions to the greater glory of God and in union with you. Finally, pray for me that I may be a sharer in the peace and joy which were yours at the hour of your death. Amen.

LITANY OF SAINT JOSEPH

Lord, have mercy on us.

Christ, have mercy on us.

Lord, have mercy on us.

Christ, hear us.

Christ, graciously hear us.

God, the Father in heaven, have mercy on us.

God the Son, Redeemer of the world, have mercy on us.

God, the Holy Spirit, have mercy on us.

Holy Trinity, one God, have mercy on us.

Holy Mary, *pray for us.*

Holy Joseph, *pray for us.*

Noble son of David, *pray for us.*
Light of the patriarchs, *pray for us.*
Spouse of the Mother of God, *pray for us.*
Chaste guardian of the Virgin, *pray for us.*
Foster father of the Son of God, *pray for us.*
Valiant defender of Christ, *pray for us.*
Head of the Holy Family, *pray for us.*
Joseph most just, *pray for us.*
Joseph most chaste, *pray for us.*
Joseph most prudent, *pray for us.*
Joseph most valiant, *pray for us.*
Joseph most obedient, *pray for us.*
Joseph most faithful, *pray for us.*
Mirror of patience, *pray for us.*
Lover of poverty, *pray for us.*
Model of workers, *pray for us.*
Ornament of domestic life, *pray for us.*
Protector of virgins, *pray for us.*
Pillar of families, *pray for us.*
Consolation of the afflicted, *pray for us.*
Hope of the sick, *pray for us.*
Patron of the dying, *pray for us.*
Terror of the demons, *pray for us.*
Protector of the holy Church, *pray for us.*

Lamb of God, who takes away the sins of the world,
    spare us, O Lord.
Lamb of God, who takes away the sins of the world,
    graciously hear us, O Lord.
Lamb of God, who takes away the sins of the world,
    have mercy on us, O Lord.

V. He gave him charge of his household.

R. And command over all his goods.

Let us pray. O God, in your providence you chose blessed Joseph to be the spouse of your most holy Mother. Grant, we implore you, that we may have him, whom we venerate on earth, as our protector in heaven. Who lives and reigns world without end. Amen.

TO SAINT JOSEPH, PATRON OF WORKERS

O Saint Joseph, model for all who work, obtain for me the grace to perform my labors in the spirit of penance, so that I may atone for my many sins. Give me the intent to work with joy, seeing it as an honor to use and develop the gifts I have received from almighty God; to work with order, peace, and moderation, giving me the intent to rise above weariness and difficulties; and to work with an eye ever on the accounting I must give at the hour of death. Keep me from empty pride in my success and from making success the centerpiece of my life. Keep me focused on the work of God in imitation of you, O Joseph. May this be my goal in life as in death. Amen.

INVOCATIONS TO SAINT JOSEPH

O blessed servant of Christ, minister of Christ incarnate, approach him for us and request the peace and safety of those who bless you.

You who were counted worthy to see Christ in the form of a human child and to be called his father, your glory and your dignity is great. Thus, we acclaim you.

Wise Joseph, you have held in your arms the child born of the Virgin, whom the powers of heaven adore as infinite God, we revere you for your holy contact with him.

Joseph Most Excellent, your life was a worthy one and now you are among the splendors of the saints. Sanctify those who faithfully honor your sacred memory.

Blessed Joseph, you who earned the praise of the Word of God, you who have approached him with confidence, pray for us always that we who proclaim your praise may be delivered from temptation.

Joseph, tell the good news that you have seen the Virgin with Child, the glad tidings that you have seen the Magi and the shepherds who have adored this Child, the marvelous message of the vision of the angel, through these glories let us receive the Word of the Lord. Entreat him that our souls be saved. Amen.

PRAYER TO SAINT JOSEPH

Blessed Joseph, we come to you in the hour of our need and implore your patronage. Through the holy charity that bound you to the Virgin Mother of God and through the fatherly love with which you embraced the Child Jesus, we beg you to take note of the inheritance that Jesus Christ has earned with his blood. O most watchful Guardian of the Holy Family, with your power and strength to aid us in our tribulations, defend us, the chosen children of Jesus Christ.

Loving Joseph, ward off from us every error and corrupting influence, assist us in our struggle with the power of darkness even as you once rescued the Child Jesus from deadly peril, and protect God's holy Church from all adversity. Shield, too, each one of us by your constant protection, so that, supported by your example and your aid, we may be able to live and die in holiness and to obtain eternal happiness in heaven. Amen.

2. Prayers to the Saints

LITANY OF THE SAINTS

Lord, have mercy. *Lord, have mercy.*
Christ, have mercy. *Christ, have mercy.*

Lord, have mercy. *Lord, have mercy.*
Christ, hear us. *Christ, hear us.*
Christ, graciously hear us. *Christ, graciously hear us.*

God, our heavenly Father, *have mercy on us.*
God the Son, Redeemer of the world, *have mercy on us.*
God the Holy Spirit, *have mercy on us.*
Holy Trinity, one God, *have mercy on us.*

Holy Mary, *pray for us.*
Holy Mother of God, *pray for us.*
Holy Virgin of virgins, *pray for us.*
Saint Michael, *pray for us.*
Saint Gabriel, *pray for us.*
Saint Raphael, *pray for us.*
All you holy angels and archangels, *pray for us.*
All you holy orders of blessed spirits, *pray for us.*

Saint John the Baptist, *pray for us.*
Saint Joseph, *pray for us.*
All you holy patriarchs and prophets, *pray for us.*

Saint Peter, *pray for us.*
Saint Paul, *pray for us.*
Saint Andrew, *pray for us.*
Saint James, *pray for us.*
Saint John, *pray for us.*
Saint Thomas, *pray for us.*
Saint Philip, *pray for us.*
Saint Bartholomew, *pray for us.*
Saint Matthew, *pray for us.*
Saint Simon, *pray for us.*

Saint Thaddeus, *pray for us.*
Saint Barnabas, *pray for us.*
Saint Luke, *pray for us.*
Saint Mark, *pray for us.*
All you holy apostles and Evangelists, *pray for us.*
All you holy disciples of the Lord, *pray for us.*
All you holy Innocents, *pray for us.*

Saint Stephen, *pray for us.*
Saint Lawrence, *pray for us.*
Saint Vincent, *pray for us.*
Saint Fabian and Saint Sebastian, *pray for us.*
Saint John and Saint Paul, *pray for us.*
Saint Cosmas and Saint Damian, *pray for us.*
Saint Gervase and Saint Protase, *pray for us.*
All you holy martyrs, *pray for us.*

Saint Sylvester, *pray for us.*
Saint Gregory, *pray for us.*
Saint Ambrose, *pray for us.*
Saint Augustine, *pray for us.*
Saint Jerome, *pray for us.*
Saint Martin, *pray for us.*
Saint Nicholas, *pray for us.*
All you holy bishops and confessors, *pray for us.*
All you holy Doctors, *pray for us.*
Saint Anthony, *pray for us.*
Saint Benedict, *pray for us.*
Saint Bernard, *pray for us.*
Saint Dominic, *pray for us.*
Saint Francis, *pray for us.*

All you holy priests and clergy, *pray for us.*
All you holy monks and hermits, *pray for us.*

Saint Mary Magdalene, *pray for us.*
Saint Agatha, *pray for us.*
Saint Lucy, *pray for us.*
Saint Agnes, *pray for us.*
Saint Cecilia, *pray for us.*
Saint Catherine, *pray for us.*
Saint Anastasia, *pray for us.*
All you holy virgins and widows, *pray for us.*
All you saints of God, *pray for us.*

Be merciful, *Lord, save your people.*
From every evil, *Lord, save your people.*
From every sin, *Lord, save your people.*
From your anger, *Lord, save your people.*
From sudden and unforeseen death, *Lord, save your people.*
From the snares of the devil, *Lord, save your people.*
From anger, hatred, and all ill will, *Lord, save your people.*
From the spirit of uncleanness, *Lord, save your people.*
From lightning and tempest, *Lord, save your people.*
From the scourge of earthquake, *Lord, save your people.*
From plague, famine, and war, *Lord, save your people.*
From everlasting death, *Lord, save your people.*
By the mystery of your holy Incarnation, *Lord, save your people.*
By your coming, *Lord, save your people.*
By your birth, *Lord, save your people.*
By your baptism and holy fasting, *Lord, save your people.*
By your Cross and suffering, *Lord, save your people.*
By your death and burial, *Lord, save your people.*
By your holy Resurrection, *Lord, save your people.*

By your wonderful ascension, *Lord, save your people.*

By the coming of the Holy Spirit, the Paraclete,
    Lord, save your people.

On the day of Judgment, *Lord, save your people.*

Be merciful to us sinners, *Lord, save your people.*

That you will spare us, *Lord, save your people.*

That you will pardon us, *Lord, save your people.*

That it may please you to bring us to true repentance,
    Lord, save your people.

To govern and preserve your holy Church, *Lord, save your people.*

To preserve in holy religion the pope,
    and all those in holy orders, *Lord, save your people.*

To humble the enemies of holy Church, *Lord, save your people.*

To give peace and unity to the whole Christian people,
    Lord, save your people.

To recall to the unity of the Church all those who are straying,
    to bring all unbelievers to the light of the gospel,
    Lord, save your people.

To strengthen and preserve us in your holy service,
    Lord, save your people.

To raise our minds to desire the things of heaven,
    Lord, save your people.

To reward all our benefactors with eternal blessings,
    Lord, save your people.

To deliver our souls from eternal damnation,
    and the souls of our brethren, kinsmen, and benefactors,
    Lord, save your people.

To give and preserve the fruits of the earth,
    Lord, save your people.

To grant eternal rest to all the faithful departed,
    Lord, save your people.

That it may please you to hear and heed us,
   Jesus, Son of the living God, *Lord, hear our prayer.*

Lamb of God, who takes away the sins of the world,
   spare us, Lord.
Lamb of God, who takes away the sins of the world,
   graciously hear us, Lord.
Lamb of God, who takes away the sins of the world,
   have mercy on us, Lord.

Christ hear us, *Christ hear us.*
Lord Jesus, hear our prayer. *Lord Jesus, hear our prayer.*
Lord, have mercy. *Lord, have mercy.*
Christ, have mercy. *Christ, have mercy.*
Lord, have mercy. *Lord, have mercy.*

PRAYER TO THE HOLY MARTYRS

Glorious champions of Jesus Christ, who have fought the battle of martyrdom and have exchanged this bitter struggle for the peace of the angels in heaven, turn your eyes on me, a poor creature beset on all sides by spiritual dangers. Amid these troubles, I call to mind your great renown.

You saints who overcame bodily torment to take heaven by storm, who vanquished the pleasures of the world and who set your eyes on heaven, look with affection on me. Add to the glory of your triumph by your intercession with God, so that I too may gain victory over the corruption of this world and its empty pomp.

Blessed warriors, what comfort, what inspiration and joy it is for us to praise you and to follow in your footsteps. Your names and memories are held sacred. You who are true champions of God hasten to help me in my weakness. Give me strength to reach the heavenly kingdom where I may rejoice with you forever. Amen.

PRAYER TO SAINT BENEDICT

Glorious patriarch, holy father Benedict, I call to mind the glorious grace our Lord bestowed on you of breathing out your last breath amid words of prayer. Even your lips exhale such fragrance that it elates all other saints with delight. I ask you to be with me at the hour of my death, as a trusty comforter, placing yourself between me and the enemies around me. Shield me by your presence so that I may avoid all the pitfalls my enemies have in store for me. Help me to safely reach the joys of eternal happiness in heaven. Amen.

SAINT GERTRUDE

PRAYER TO SAINT THÉRÈSE OF LISIEUX

O admirable Saint Thérèse of the Child Jesus, who in your brief life on earth became a mirror of angelic purity and wholehearted surrender to God, now that you are enjoying your reward in heaven, look with kindness on us who put our trust in you. Obtain for us the grace to keep our hearts and minds ever pure and to detest all that can degrade, even in a small way, a virtue that so delights your heavenly Bridegroom. Dear saint, benefit us with your powerful intercession; bring us comfort in all the bitter moments of life, so that we may be able to share eternal happiness with you in paradise. Amen.

Pray for us, Saint Thérèse, that we may become worthy of the promises of Christ. Amen.

PRAYER TO SAINT ANNE, THE MOTHER OF MARY

God, who was pleased to impart such a grace upon most blessed Anne that she became worthy to bear in her womb your Blessed Mother Mary, at the intercession of them both, grant us your abundant mercy, so that by the prayers of the mother and the daughter, whose memory we cherish, we may come to our home in heaven. Amen.

PRAYER TO SAINT VINCENT DE PAUL

Saint Vincent, patron of all charitable associations and father of all those in distress, you who never in your lifetime refused anyone who appealed to you for help, see what difficulties now beset us and come quickly to our rescue. Obtain from the Lord relief for the poor, care for the sick, comfort for the afflicted, protection for the abandoned, a spirit of generosity for the rich, the conversion of sinners, peace for all nations, and salvation for all. Let all people, wherever they are, feel the effects of your merciful intercession, so that we may be united with you in the life to come. Amen.

PRAYER TO SAINT JUDE

Saint Jude, apostle of Christ, and patron of hopeless and difficult causes, pray for us in our need. Employ on our behalf, we ask of you, your powerful ability to bring speedy and suitable assistance where and when help is needed. Notwithstanding this request, help us to see our trials as reflections of the sufferings of Christ. Let us see even now the great hope and faith that we may share with Christ in the glory of his Resurrection. Intercede, however, for us in our present needs if it is God's desire that our difficulty be taken from us. We know that our prayers will be heard through your noble intercession. Through Christ our Lord. Amen.

PRAYER TO SAINT TERESA OF ÁVILA

Saint Teresa, beloved bride of our crucified Lord, you burned with such an intense love for your God and mine, and you shine brighter now in paradise. You who longed to see him loved by all people, obtain for me also a spark of that same holy fire. Help me to forget the world and all created things but also to forget even myself. Intercede for me so that our Sovereign Good will ensure that my every thought, desire, and affection may be continually directed to following, in grief and in joy, the will of God. Obtain for me this grace, you who are so powerful with God. May I be all on fire like you, blessed Doctor, with divine love. Amen.

NOVENA PRAYER TO SAINT ANTHONY, THE WONDER-WORKER

O glorious wonder-worker, Saint Anthony, father of the poor and comforter of the troubled, gentlest of saints, your love for God and charity for his creatures made you worthy, when on earth, to possess miraculous powers. Miracles waited on your word, which you were ready to speak for those in trouble or anxiety. Encouraged by this thought, I implore of you to obtain for me my request. (*Here privately speak your intention.*) The answer to my prayer may require a miracle, even so, you are the saint of miracles. O gentle and loving Saint Anthony, whose heart was ever full of human sympathy, whisper my petitions into the ears of the Sweet Infant Jesus, who loved to be folded in your arms; and the gratitude of my heart will be ever yours. Amen.

NOVENA OF GRACE TO SAINT FRANCIS XAVIER

O Saint Francis Xavier, well loved and full of charity, in union with you, I reverently adore the majesty of God. And I rejoice in the singular gifts of grace given to you during your life, and your gifts of glory after death.

I beg you with all my heart's devotion to be pleased to obtain for me, by your powerful intercession, above all things, the grace of a holy life and a happy death. Moreover, I beg of you to obtain for me (*Here speak of the intention you wish to pray for.*)....

But if what I ask of you so earnestly does not tend to the glory of God and the greater good of my soul, I pray that you obtain for me what is more profitable to both these ends. Amen.

3. Prayers to the Holy Angels

TO THE ARCHANGEL GABRIEL

Mighty of God, holy Gabriel, who made known to the Virgin Mary the incarnation of God's only Son, and who brought comfort and strength to support Christ during his agony in the garden, I praise you and I ask you to plead my cause before Jesus Christ and his blessed Mother. In all my troubles bring me strength and courage so that I may never yield to any temptation and thus offend God who is my supreme good.

Minister of God's eternal glory, obtain for us all that will be for our lasting good. We joyously sing your praise, dear Gabriel, since it was you who foretold the coming of the Word of God into mortal flesh. Therefore, we honor you and will honor you forever. Amen.

TO THE ARCHANGEL RAPHAEL

Heavenly healer and companion, holy Raphael, who restored the eyesight of the elder Tobias and who brought his son unharmed to his journey's end, heal my body and soul! Dispel the darkness of ignorance, be at my side on this hazardous pilgrimage of life, and bring me at last to that heavenly country where I may share your bliss and see God face to face. Amen.

TO ONE'S GUARDIAN ANGEL

Hail, holy angel of God, guardian of my soul and body. By the sweet heart of Jesus, Son of God, for the love of him who created you and me, for the love of him who entrusted me to you at baptism, take me under your most faithful wing, so that with your help I may cross the treacherous stream of mortal life and happily arrive with you in heaven where we may gaze on the beauty of our sovereign God with delight. Amen.

TO MICHAEL, THE ARCHANGEL

Merciful God, send to us Michael, the prince of the heavenly host, to deliver us from the power of our enemies and conduct us unscathed into your presence, our Lord and God. We know how high in your favor he has been exalted. May he ever be at hand to help us with his intercession, so that we may be alive with every virtue and have our names, with the record of our penitence, inscribed in the book of everlasting life.

O Michael, heavenly spirit, we fly with confidence to the shelter of your wings. Watch over and protect us as long as we live, and at the hour of our death come to our rescue, O friend of all humankind. Amen.

TO THE ANGEL WHO STRENGTHENED OUR LORD IN THE GARDEN OF OLIVES

I salute you, holy Angel, who comforted my Lord in his agony—the one who is the comfort and strength of all the afflicted. You are honored for the obedience, humility, and love with which you assisted Jesus when he was fainting in sorrow at seeing the sins of the world and especially mine. I ask you to obtain for me perfect sorrow for my sins and strengthen me in my own afflictions which now threaten to overwhelm me. Comfort me as well in all the other trials to which I shall be exposed in the future and, in particular, when I find myself in my own final agony. Amen.

Prayers for Friends, for Family, and for Special Intentions

1. Prayers for Friends and Family

POPE JOHN PAUL II'S PRAYER FOR FAMILIES

Lord God, from you every family in heaven and on earth takes its name. Father, you are Love and Life.

Through your Son, Jesus Christ, born of a woman, and through the Holy Spirit, fountain of divine charity, grant that every family on earth may become for each successive generation a true shrine of life and love.

Grant that your grace may guide the thoughts and actions of husbands and wives for the good of their families and of all the families of the world. Grant that the young may find in the family solid support for their human dignity and for their growth in truth and love. Grant that love, strengthened by the grace of the sacrament of marriage, may prove mightier than all the weaknesses and trials through which our families must sometimes pass.

Through the intercession of the Holy Family of Nazareth, we ask this of you, who are Life, Truth, and Love, with the Son and the Holy Spirit. Amen.

FOR FAMILY AND FRIENDS

O Lord, remember my friends, all who have prayed for me and all who have done good for me.

Return this good to them, as well as all of their kindnesses, a hundredfold. Reward them with your blessings and sanctify them with your grace.

Let all my family and relatives, my neighbors and friends, receive the benefit of the prayers I have said for them. May they also receive the unstinting support of your divine providence and the sanctification of your Holy Spirit. Amen.

215

PRAYER OF PARENTS FOR THEIR CHILDREN

Lord God, we commend our children to you. We place them in your care and protection, hoping that they will grow day by day in love for you. May they lead a good life and bring comfort to you who are their Creator.

Consider, Lord, the world in which they will pass their lives, its corruption and false allure. Be on the watch, dear Lord, to help and defend them. Lead them to the practice of virtue and the observance of your commandments. Make our lives holy also so that we may be a influential pattern for them.

We ask of you, from the bottom of our heart, your blessing on our children. We dedicate them to you, Lord; protect them as one protects the apple of his eye. Keep them in the shadow of your wings. Arrange it so that we and they may come together in heaven and praise you, most loving Father, for you have taken care of our whole family. Amen.

AN OLD PRAYER FOR FRIENDS

Blessed Mother of those whose names you can read in my heart, watch over them with every care. Make their way easy and their labors fruitful. Dry their tears if they weep; sanctify their joys; raise their courage if they weaken; restore their hope if they lose heart, their health if they become ill, truth to their hearts if they fall into error, and repentance if they fall into sin. Amen.

PRAYER FOR ONE'S ENEMIES

Almighty God, have mercy on my enemies and all who bear me ill will and wish me harm. Have mercy on their faults and on mine as well. Through your tender plan for harmony and mercy, and using such means as your infinite wisdom will devise, amend our conduct and redress any wrongs that have been done, and grant us to be saved souls in heaven together, where we may ever live and love you and your blessed saints, through the bitter passion of our Savior and the glory of the Holy Trinity. Amen.

SAINT THÉRÈSE OF LISIEUX'S PRAYER FOR CHILDREN

O Eternal Father, your only-begotten Son, the dear Child Jesus, belongs to me, since you have given him.

I offer you the infinite merits of his divine childhood. I ask you, in his name, to open the gates of heaven to a countless host of little children, who will, forever, follow this Holy Lamb. Amen.

FOR LOVED ONES WHO ARE ABSENT

O God, we thank you for the love we have for those who are absent from us, and whose love neither time nor space can diminish. We thank you that those who are absent from us are still present with you. We trust them to your loving care, knowing that underneath are the everlasting arms, only beseeching you to grant that both they and we, by drawing nearer to you, may be drawn nearer to one another, through Christ, our Lord. Amen.

PRAYER FOR LOVE OF NEIGHBOR

Lord Jesus, you teach that the greatest of all virtues is love. I heartily ask for an expansion of love for my neighbor. Give me a love that is patient, long-suffering, kind and nonjudgmental and, above all, not self-seeking, envious, or irritable.

Let my love take no notice of injury, real or imagined, and refuse to rejoice when injustice triumphs. Rather, let my love be joyful when truth prevails. Create in me a love that is always ready to make allowances and that trusts and hopes. May my love be kind, merciful, and forgiving in imitation of your Father's love for me. Amen.

PRAYER FOR A HAPPY HOME

Dear Father, we thank you for our home and our safe passage. We thank you for giving us to one another in this family and for our joys and blessings that we have shared. We thank you for our shared happiness and the comfort we afford one another in times of sorrow. We ask you to increase our love for one another and to continue to serve them with a generous spirit. We hope that we will be ready to help each other in our daily cares and work with eagerness, truth, and honesty. Lord, may we always face the world united and supportive of one another. Grant that our quarrels and petty annoyances be quickly forgiven or forgotten. Hear our prayer, and grant that your presence always be felt in our home and in our hearts. Amen.

2. Prayers for Special Intentions

FOR THE HUNGRY

Make us worthy, O Lord, to serve our fellow human beings throughout the world who live and die in hunger and poverty. Give them through our hands this day their daily bread, and by our understanding give them love, peace, and joy. Amen.

MOTHER TERESA OF CALCUTTA

PRAYER FOR PEACE IN OUR TIMES

Give peace in our times, O Lord, because there is none other that fights for us, but only you, O Lord our God.

V. Peace be within your walls.
R. And abundance within your towers.

Let us pray: O God, from whom all holy desires, all wisdom, and all just works proceed, give to your children that peace which the world cannot give, so that our hearts may be employed to obey your commandments, and so that we who are thus delivered from the fear of our enemies, may spend our time under your protection, in rest and quietude, through Christ our Lord. Amen.

PRAYER FOR SOCIAL JUSTICE

Lord Jesus, carpenter and king, supreme sovereign of all peoples, look with mercy and compassion on all the many peoples of our day who must endure the indignities of injustice. Raise up leaders in every time and place who are dedicated to your standards of order, equity, and justice. Grant to us, Lord Jesus, the grace to be members of your Church, and work unceasingly to fulfill our vocation in its social apostolate. Sharpen our intellects to cut through the pettiness of prejudice, to perceive the beauty of true human community. Guide our minds to a useful understanding of the problems of the poor, of the oppressed, of the unemployed, the marginalized, and of all in need of assistance anywhere. Guard our hearts against the subtle guile of earthly things and undue admiration for those who possess them. May we always hunger and thirst after justice. Amen.

PRAYER FOR CHURCH UNITY

God our Father, it is your purpose to bring the whole of creation into unity with you. Give us the grace to further this aim and to live out your truth on earth. Bring all your people closer to one another and unite us in the sharing of your good news. Come, Holy Spirit, and help us join into one community of believers. Amen.

PRAYER FOR VOCATIONS

Jesus, High Priest and Redeemer forever, we beg you to call young men and women to your service as priests and religious. May they be inspired by the lives of dedicated priests, brothers, and sisters. Give to their parents the grace of generosity and trust toward you and their children so that their sons and daughters may be helped to choose their vocations in life with wisdom and freedom.

Lord, you told us that the harvest indeed is great but the laborers are few. Pray, therefore, the Lord of the harvest, to send laborers into his harvest. We ask that we may know and follow the vocation to which you have called us. We pray particularly for those called to serve as priests, brothers, and sisters; those whom you have called, those you are calling now, and those you will call in the future. May they be open and responsive to the call of serving your people. We ask this through Christ, our Lord. Amen.

PRAYER FOR THE SANCTITY OF LIFE

Lord God, the giver of life, at whose command all creation was given birth, teach us to reverence life and sanctify it. Let us rejoice that every human life is sacred, whether it belongs to those close at hand or those who live far away, whether it belongs to an unborn infant or one who is terminally ill. Remind us that each individual has been redeemed by your Son, Jesus Christ; let us celebrate the existence of each and every person and preserve all life from harm or degradation. Amen.

FOR THE SETTLEMENT OF DISPUTES

God the Creator, who made our complex world of relationships, preserve the delicate balance of human interactions. Grant that all those involved in disputes will be inclined to listen to one another rather than to find fault, that each side will offer respect to one another rather than suspicion, and that solutions that are just for all concerned may be reached in harmony and good will, through Jesus Christ, our Lord. Amen.

IN TIME OF DISASTER

God and Father of us all, hear our prayer. We look to you with hope in the midst of this disaster. Bring comfort and help to all whose homes have been darkened by this tragedy. Help the injured and bereaved find solace. Raise up good men and women to offer their generous aid fully and freely and bless their efforts and strengthen their resolve. We ask you this through Christ, our Lord. Amen.

Brief Manual of Ways to Pray

*T*here are many paths to prayer but only one goal: union with God. Here is a brief outline of possible prayer strategies that may offer options to those who wish to explore varying prayer practices.

1. Forms of Prayer According to Content

PRAYER OF THANKSGIVING

In prayers of thanksgiving we give gratitude to God for his very act of creation and his work in our own lives and the lives of others. We identify God's gifts and blessings and give thanks with a grateful heart. This act of gratitude leads us to a more generous gift of ourselves to God and a deeper relationship with him. Prayers of thanksgiving encourage the acknowledgment of our absolute dependence on God and reminds us that the blessings in this life are not the result of our own hard work and talent.

How, then, should we give thanks to God for his wonderful blessings? We can do this in many ways:

- Pray the psalms of thanksgiving, for example, Psalm 116.
- Give thanks to God not necessarily for the good things that happen but *in the face of* all things that happen.
- Attend a special celebration of the holy Mass as a prayer of thanksgiving.
- Use the beads of the rosary as counters to recite our reasons to be thankful to God.
- Offer specific actions of thanksgiving by sharing our blessings with others. We could thank God for our good fortune by sharing our material blessings with others less fortunate. We could thank God for the gift of our education by tutoring those who are learning to read. We could give thanks to God for our health by visiting the sick and offering our ongoing assistance.

- Search for and compile prayers of thanksgiving authored by others that reflect our own gratitude.
- During morning prayer, give thanks for one blessing from God that happened the day before.

PRAYER OF PETITION

In prayers of petition, we ask God to do something for us or to give something to us. On the surface, petitionary prayer seems simple; it was probably the earliest form of prayer and one that Jesus used often in the New Testament. Despite all the theological questions associated with prayers of petition (Do we petition God in order to make him change his mind? Are prayers of petition effective in so far as God has already ordered the events of our world?), these kinds of prayers are deep and authentic expressions of faith and trust in God; repeating and persevering in prayer of petition is a constant renewal of our hope in God.

Prayers of petition are also a response to God's invitation to us to "Call on me in time of calamity; I will deliver you" (Ps 50:15). God asks us to call on him to seek from him what we need to live our lives in peace. We pray, not out of pure selfishness, but in response to God's own initiative.

How, then, should we petition God for his help? Here are some ways:

- Ask God's help whenever the impulse strikes during the day. Do not be afraid to make your petition, for our Lord has said: "And so I say to you, 'Ask and it will be given to you; seek and you will find; knock and it will be opened to you'" (Lk 11:9).
- Underpin prayers of petition with an absolute belief in God's interest in us—an interest that has already been proven. This makes God our good friend rather than some wealthy benefactor who merely dispenses "goodies."

- Recognize God's granting of our prior petitions and ask for help in recognizing his answers to our prayers.
- Petition for the "big" things: in fact, make a prayer list of requests and keep it up-to-date. The big things are (1) discovering and embracing God's will for us; (2) help in becoming the persons God created us to be; (3) guidance in finding a deeper love for the Father, Son, and Holy Spirit; (4) increase in love for the people in our lives, each and every one; (5) assistance in using the gifts of time, treasure, and talent more effectively; (6) help in surviving the onslaughts of sin.
- Ask in faith, for our Lord said, "Whatever you ask for in prayer full of faith, you will receive" (Mt 21:22).

PRAYER OF INTERCESSION

In prayers of intercession, we ask God to do something for or give something to another person. Prayers of intercession are examples of our deepest compassion for others; they are true gifts. As Jesuit Anthony de Mello says:

> It is only at the end of this world that we shall realize how the destinies of persons and nations have been shaped, not so much by the external actions of powerful men and by events that seemed inevitable, but the quiet, silent, irresistible prayer of persons the world will never know.

Prayers of intercession bring benefits back to the persons who offer them. Surprisingly, as we reach out in compassionate intercession for the needs of others, God quietly takes care of our own needs.

How, then, should we ask God to intercede in his mercy for others? Here are some ways:

- Follow Saint Paul's advice: "Do not be anxious about anything. In everything resort to prayer and supplication together with thanksgiving and bring your requests before God. Then the peace of God, which surpasses all understanding, will keep your hearts and minds in Christ Jesus" (Phil 4:6–7).

- Choose something you often struggle with (for example, envy, a physical ailment, intemperate language, or other difficulty) and intercede for someone else with a similar difficulty.

- Read the newspaper and intercede for one person whose difficulties are recorded there.

- Stand in for another person and receive the holy Eucharist for him or her.

- Create a prayer basket and write down the names and needs of people, putting them in the prayer basket and trusting that God will take care of them.

- Pick a certain group of people to pray for: priests and religious; parish renewal; married couples; citizens of countries experiencing armed conflicts, natural disasters, or other calamities; all sick children; those with incurable diseases, and so on.

- Intercede for those who need reconciliation: those estranged from the Church, those who feel abandoned by God, those who harbor prejudice against others, and so on.

PRAYER OF CONTRITION OR EXAMINATION OF CONSCIENCE

In prayers of contrition, we seek God's gift of sorrow for our sins—its ugliness, its destructiveness, its false allure, its shroud of alienation—and hope for our return to the mercy of God. As the epistle says, "If we say, 'We have no sin,' we deceive ourselves and the truth is not in us. If we confess our sins, he who is faithful and just will forgive us our sins and cleanse us from all wickedness" (1 Jn 1:8–9).

Father Eamon Tobin, C.Ss.R, gives us a plan to achieve prayer of contrition. He outlines five actions to encourage contrition: (1) Pray frequently for the gift of a contrite heart; (2) Pray for the grace to exterminate some sinful behavior in our lives. (Father Tobin recommends the frequent small, specific prayers, which may have to be said for a lifetime, as a tool.); (3) Pray to truly experience the mercy of our loving Father; (4) Humbly and often thank God for his mercy, for we are totally dependent on God; (5) Pray for true contrition, for authentic reconciliation with God and with the members of our own believing community.

How, then, should we pray the prayer of contrition? Here are some ways:

Consciousness Examen: This is a spiritual exercise popularized by Saint Ignatius of Loyola. Part of the purpose of this effort is to grow in sensitive awareness to the voice of the Holy Spirit, who guides us to the truth about ourselves and our sins. It also helps us discern how our weaknesses and our sinful side pull us away from the Father's call and lead us to a life of self-gratification. Here are three steps to follow:

- Start by praying to the Holy Spirit to help us see the events of the day accurately and in the light of his counsel.
- Choose a particular event or encounter of the day and focus on it. When we decide on a particular event, we should then evaluate what was really happening. Were our attitudes and behavior Christ-centered? Were we being true to God's will or were we acting indifferently? Was our day Christ-centered, other-centered, or completely self-centered? Were the people we met treated as Christ-bearers or were they seen as mere utilitarian tools for personal use? What are we doing with the "garden" God has entrusted to us?
- Offer prayers of contrition and repentance.

Examination of Conscience: A daily tally of sins conducted periodically and as preparation for the reception of the sacrament of penance. The very act of conducting an examination of conscience is in itself a prayer. A traditionally formulated examination of conscience begins on page 55 of this book. What follows is another set of categories that might be useful in conducting a personal inventory. These are based on a set of values statements listed by Philip St. Romain in his book *Twelve Steps to Spiritual Wholeness: A Christian Pathway* (Liguori, MO: Liguori Publications, 1992).

Values From the Ten Commandments: (1) Putting God first; (2) Reverence for the name of God; (3) Keeping holy the Lord's day; (4) Respect for parents; (5) Restraint from violence toward others; (6) Chastity in sexual relationships; (7) Honesty in dealing with others; (8) Honesty in speech; (9) Fidelity in relationships; (10) Being content with material possessions.

Values From the Cardinal Virtues: (1) Moderation in the use of food, drink, material goods; (2) Taking responsibility for meeting your own needs; (3) Working for justice; (4) Standing up for your beliefs.

Values From the Works of Mercy: (1) Helping those in need of food, drink, clothing, shelter; (2) Visiting the sick; (3) Visiting prisoners; (4) Forgiving others the wrongs done to you; (5) Exercising patience; (6) Comforting others when they are troubled.

Healing of Past Sins: Examine your past sins and choose one for which you still feel completely unreconciled. Imagine a merciful Jesus with you. Talk to him about this sinful behavior and ask for his fuller forgiveness and healing.

PRAYER OF DISCERNMENT OR DECISION-MAKING

In prayers of discernment, we ask God's divine guidance in making a decision. Jesus promised us the gift of his Spirit: "I will ask the Father and he will give you another helper to be with you forever, [the] Spirit of truth" (Jn 14:16–17), the Holy Spirit who leads us closer to God.

Prayers of discernment are like conversations with an intimate friend; they are personal interchanges whose goal is to seek the will of God. Prayers of discernment accomplished through the Holy Spirit and accompanied by a conscious and sincere effort to know and heed the will of God (not a mistaken assumption of our own will *disguised as* God's) become a path to greater spiritual maturity and closer communion with our Creator.

Even though God does not have a direct telephone line to us when we are seeking discernment, there is a prayerful process that can help us hear his voice more clearly:

- Create a specific statement of what we are trying to decide.
- Set out the pros and cons of each alternative and identify that alternative to which we feel most drawn.
- Assemble the information and bring it to prayer, asking for God's guidance. As we pray, we ask for the grace of inner freedom to walk down any path that the Lord directs. If we are so attached to a particular option, we are really not free to move in another direction. Ideally, we should not choose any path unless we become so detached that we are able to choose every path.

Saint Ignatius of Loyola has three exercises that may aid us in evaluating our options: (1) We should consider what advice we would give to another person faced with the same situation; (2) We can imagine ourselves on our deathbed and ask what we would then wish to have chosen; (3) We can picture ourselves standing before God on the Judgment Day and ask ourselves what decision we would then wish to have made.

- Make a decision, choosing the alternative that gives us the most peace when we are in prayer. Take enough time to imagine how you would react to actually living that decision.
- Live with the decision, praying again for God's direction.
- Act on the decision we have made with God's help, even if we experience a pull in some other direction.
- Seek counsel and confirmation of the decision from trustworthy and spiritually mature advisors.

PRAYER OF FORGIVENESS

The *Catechism* is quite clear: Forgiveness (of self and others) is a prerequisite for both the Eucharistic Liturgy and for personal prayer (*CCC* §2631). Further, the Gospel of Luke says, "But I say to you who hear me: Love your enemies, do good to those who hate you. Bless those who curse you and pray for those who treat you badly" (Lk 6:27–28); while Mark says, "And when you stand to pray, forgive whatever you may hold against anyone" (Mk 11:25).

Forgiveness prayer is not just letting bygones be bygones or the resigned martyrdom of "giving it up." It is a pathway through the anger, resentment, and blame to a loving God. Father Eamon Tobin, in his book *How to Forgive Yourself and Others* (Liguori, MO: Liguori Publication, 1993), lists eight factors about forgiveness that ought to be considered by anyone attempting to let go of the hurt and blame: (1) Forgiveness is God's way of dealing with life's hurts; only he gives us the grace to let these hurts go; (2) Forgiveness happens only when we truly desire it; (3) Frequently we bury the fact that we really *do not want* to forgive; only God's grace will help us uncover our secret hostility; (4) Forgiveness of a hurt takes time and patience; (5) Remember that we hurt others ordinarily because we are weak and ignorant, not because we are filled with malicious evil and cold-blooded cruelty. This same fact goes for those who hurt us; (6) Forgiveness is essentially an act of the will and not a matter of feelings; if we continue to act in negative ways, it is a sign that we have not truly forgiven; (7) There is a difference between forgiveness and reconciliation; with God's grace, we can always forgive, but we cannot always reconcile a relationship to its past status; (8) We may have a difficult time with forgiveness if we have a difficult time forgiving ourselves; if we cannot receive from others and from God their forgiveness, how can we offer it to others?

How, then, should we say the prayer of forgiveness? Here are some ways:

- Pray through the pain, asking God to give you the grace to forgive. Repent of any contributory wrongdoing on your part and judgmentalism. Pray for the person who has hurt you. Do some act of goodness to the person you have forgiven or to someone who has caused a similar hurt to you.
- Prayerfully give a financial contribution in honor of the person you are forgiving.
- Pray to God for unqualified forgiveness with no reservations or "hold backs."
- Make a forgiveness list. Pray for those who make your life difficult: bosses, in-laws, or siblings. Pray for world leaders, especially those whose politics are not in agreement with yours. Pray for the "baddies": murderers, thieves, rapists, child molesters, liars, polluters of the environment.

2. Prayer Forms According to Complexity

VOCAL PRAYER

In vocal prayer, we pray publicly with liturgical celebrations (the Mass), privately with prayers of our own choice, with our own words, or the set words of others. Vocal prayer is prayer that takes form in words. We are bodily creatures who need the experience of expressing our inner prayer impulses in an external and concrete way. Vocal prayer is probably the most familiar form of prayer and the one that we learn first. Jesus encouraged the use of vocal prayer in that the prayer he taught his disciples, the Our Father, is an example of vocal prayer. Vocal prayer is sometimes distinguished from mental prayer which is not tied to any set formulas.

How, then, should we approach the art of vocal prayer? Here are some ways:

- Collect examples of powerful prayers written by the spiritual masters: the saints, the Fathers and Doctors of the Church, modern spiritual writers who strike a chord in our emotions. Keep these volumes close at hand for use when this type of prayer is chosen or when you want to fall back on the words of others.

- Choose vocal prayers to match your moods, emotionally or spiritually. Say each prayer with reflection and concentration. Truly mean the words and make them your own.

- Allow time to be recollected before beginning vocal prayer. Do not rush in and recite vocal prayers with a rote mind-set.

- Use vocal prayers as a model, creating prayers in your own words. Make these prayers truly your own.

- Recall always that these prayers are in reality person-to-person communication with God. Always remember to whom these vocal prayers are addressed; do not just throw the words out spiritlessly.

PRAYER OF HOLY READING OR *LECTIO DIVINA*

Praying the prayer of holy reading is a very ancient form of prayer, one as old as Christendom. Even before the time of Jesus, the Jewish rabbis said that God's law was his presence to which we open ourselves through reading, meditation, and prayer. Christendom inherited this way of scriptural prayer from Judaism, and it was taken over by the monastic tradition in which this form of reading was always mixed with inner prayer. Saint Bernard of Clairvaux writes concerning Scriptures that "from the daily reading every day, a mouthful can go down into the memory's stomach in order to be digested better." Though the Scriptures are by far the most common book used for holy reading, other spiritual works of the Doctors and Fathers of the Church are also used in this way.

How, then, should we approach the art of *lectio divina*? Here are some suggestions:

- Wilfrid Stinissen, author of *Nourished by the Word: Reading the Bible Contemplatively* (Liguori, MO: Liguori Publications, 1999), recommends an active variant of *lectio* used by Charles de Foucauld (1858–1916). In this method, one writes a short meditation, preferably in the form of prayer, on a Bible text. Charles de Foucauld actually installed a table before the altar in the chapel, and there wrote down his meditations. This method is useful since there is a risk that the biblical texts no longer speak to us because we have heard and read them so often.
- Father Basil Pennington, OCSO, sums up the practice of *lectio divina* in this way: (1) Keep the sacred Scriptures in the home in a place of honor and regard it as the real presence of the

Word in your midst; (2) Take up the Bible with reverence and pray to the Holy Spirit for enlightened reading and listening; (3) For five minutes (or longer, is you so wish), listen to the Lord speaking to you through the text and respond to him; (4) At the end of the time, choose a word or phrase (perhaps one will have forcefully been called to your attention) to take with you and thank the Lord for being with you and speaking to you.

- Use the words of the Bible to create your own spontaneous prayers inspired by the texts you are reading.

MEDITATION

Praying meditatively demands a concentrated attentiveness to discovering what God wants of us and what response we need to make to his divine will. Meditation is prayer in which the intellect and reason are dominant. Meditation is a conscious effort to place oneself in the presence of God and to foster attitudes of faith, praise, and abandonment to divine will. The exercise of meditation is usually focused or guided by written material such as a Scripture passage or notes from spiritual reading.

In the monastic tradition, the practice of *lectio divina* was the beginning of a process that included meditation (*meditatio*), affective prayer (*oratio*), and contemplation (*contemplatio*). Today when we speak of meditation, we are usually thinking of a more rational than emotional process employing the mind and the imagination, which seeks to break through the literal words and events to the thoughts and images beyond them. We look instead in a informed way, letting the fullness of the reality impress itself on us.

How, then, should we approach praying meditatively? Here is a procedure from Abbot Michael Casey that is found in his book *Toward God: The Ancient Wisdom of Western Prayer* (Liguori, MO: Liguori Publications, 1996):

- Give yourself time to slow down and clear your head for meditation. At the regular time you have selected for meditation, go to your prayer place and either kneel, sit, or assume some other prayerful posture.

- Make a formal beginning with the Sign of the Cross or a brief opening prayer. Then recite slowly and reverently the short prayer selected for this session. Do not think about its meaning and try to analyze it. Simply give yourself to saying it and repeating it a few times.

- As the prayer starts to slow down, pick up a text or other means of focusing the meditation session. If one idea or part stands out, devote most of your time and attention to that.

- Feel the meditative prayer coming from your heart, and arising slowing from the situation in which you find yourself before God. Let it lead you.

- Allow the sense of spiritual presence to strengthen. Encourage whatever reinforces this presence. Allow the prayerful presence to dictate the direction of the meditative session.

- If other distracting thoughts come along, lead them gently away. If necessary remove them by returning to the short prayer.

- As you sense that your meditation is complete, gently wind matters up. Perhaps you may wish to close with a formal prayer or add some word of intercession. Wait for a few minutes and then return to other daily activities.

CONTEMPLATION

Contemplative prayer is a gazing upon Christ: a gazing that has no need for words, thoughts, or ideas. Contemplation is present when we stop reading (*lectio*), thinking (*meditatio*), and speaking (*oratio*), and begin resting silently in the Lord's presence. The contemplative form of prayer for a long time seemed to signify an experience that was only open to a few privileged religious and monks. It now has come to be seen as an experience that can normally flow out of our baptism. Contemplation is not about words; above all, it is about love.

The Trappist monk Thomas Merton, who did much to bring the prayer of contemplation into ordinary awareness, describes it in this way:

Contemplative prayer is, in a way, simply the preference for the desert, for emptiness, for poverty. One has begun to know the meaning of contemplation when he intuitively and spontaneously seeks the dark and unknown path of aridity in preference to any other way. The contemplative is one who would rather not know than know. Rather not enjoy than enjoy. Rather not have *proof* that God loves him.

THOMAS MERTON, *THE CLIMATE OF MONASTIC PRAYER*

Nurturing a contemplative attitude is an important adjunct to contemplative prayer. Some contemplatives have given these kinds of advice to achieve that end: (1) Foster loving rather than analyzing God; (2) Create both deep interior and exterior silence; (3) A contemplative attitude is fostered by an openness to and love of others; (4) Self-denial and sacrifice free us for contemplative prayer; (5) Simplify your life in order to achieve a resolute attention to God; (6) Cultivate the "dark night of the soul," for it is through this that we leave our souls in the hands of God.

How, then, should we go about praying contemplatively? Here is a method recommended by Joyce Huggett in her book *Learning the Language of Prayer:*

- First, enter your place of prayer and relax in the presence of God, granting to him the gift of your time and attention. If you are tense, recognize some of the reasons why: stress of your job, worries about your children, the pressure of things that need to be done. Hand over all these things to God.
- Slip slowly into an awareness of the presence of God. Seek the fresh air of an awareness of the greatness, splendor, and gentleness of God. As this attitude becomes more second-nature to us, our spiritual energy will increase.
- Surrender every part of ourselves to God: your body, mind, and emotions; your desires, plans, and intentions; every relationship, your work, your day, your heart.
- Open yourself to God's healing love and let him heal the deepest and most chronic sickness of your soul. Close your eyes and be aware of the Lord's giving you his own gift of peace: peace of mind, peace of heart, peace with yourself; peace with everyone.
- Let the Lord take the burdens and sufferings of the present, and at the same time entrust your whole future to him.
- With this preparation, we are ready for a period of contemplation. Joyce Huggett describes contemplation in this way:

In the quietness, aware of his presence, we open our hearts to receive his love. The prayer is usually wordless and fed by a deep desire for him. This leads us on to a place where instead of seeking God, we are found by him. We discover that, long before we came to our place of prayer, he was seeking us. So he responds to our longing. We bask in the warmth of his love. We feel his gaze on us. He fills us afresh with his Spirit. We receive a new perspective on life—his perspective.

3. Prayer in Varying Contexts

PRAYER IN SOLITUDE

Praying in solitude means purposefully giving up our normal activities and interactions with people for a time in order to forgo our external securities and rest in the strength of the Lord. Jesus needed, as do we, solitude to do the work of his Father; for example, the Gospel of Mark says: "Very early in the morning, before daylight, Jesus went off to a lonely place where he prayed" (Mk 1:35).

Part of solitude is attaining silence, or a quiet, still state, free from all intrusive mental activity that is not rooted in God. Spiritual writer Henri Nouwen has said: "Without solitude, it is virtually impossible to live a spiritual life."

A time-honored way to spend quality time nurturing our relationship with God is to allocate time for a retreat. The time for a retreat may vary from one or two hours over several days, to a single day, to several weeks or several months. The place of a retreat may vary from a place set aside in your own home to a formal retreat center whose special purpose is conducting retreats.

Another devotional practice—arising from Russian tradition—is a *poustinia*: a solitary place where one might go for meditation on a regular basis. Catherine de Hueck Doherty, founder of Madonna House, describes an ideal poustinia: it should be a simple, plain room, containing a Bible, a chair and a table, some writing paper and pencils. If there is a bed it should have wooden slats instead of a mattress, with a few blankets and a pillow if necessary. Hot water for tea or coffee could be acceptable. The only other artifacts in the room would be a cross and/or other religious picture, along with a vigil light. Doherty also describes the elements required of periodic withdrawal to a poustinia: (1) Understand that silence leads to contemplation; (2) Know that true silence is listening to God; (3) Spend time in a poustinia on a regular basis; (4) Listen for a word from God; (5) Prepare in advance for solitude by calming the mind, closing the intellect, and opening the heart; (6) Enter solitude knowing that you are in the mind of God; (7) Empty the self.

Another important time of praying in solitude involves the reception of the holy Eucharist. It is then that we are most truly in communication with God and it is a time of prayer par excellence. At this time, you may wish to plan on concentrating totally on treating the Lord as a close and trusted friend. In addition, you may wish to select a word from the Gospels or other prayer of the day's Mass and use that word as a springboard for discussion with the Lord. Daily or weekly, our most important prayer time is this one wherein we make Jesus Christ welcome and give him our full attention. Further, it is a good idea to pray on the way to Mass (for oneself, the priest, the parish) and to stay after Mass to continue conversation with our Lord.

SHARED PRAYER

The most important shared prayer is our participation in the liturgy of the Church. Bishop Robert Morneau says that prayer is a way to internalize and assimilate the liturgy and a way to draw us into communion with God and with one another. It is a way of saying "I bring to Mass all that I am and love. I come away enriched and energized to further God's kingdom" (*Paths to Prayer*, Cincinnati, OH: St. Anthony Messenger Press, 1998).

The partner of personal prayer is always this public expression of faith in the context of community. The liturgical worship of the Church keeps us in constant remembrance of the life, death, and Resurrection of Jesus, as we journey annually through the seasons of the Church's year. We need the prayer of community to provide support in our joys and sorrows (baptism, marriage, funerals) and solidarity in our faith as members of the Mystical Body of Christ.

Another way of practicing communal prayer is in the context of small-group sharing. This prayer format was very normal for the first followers of Jesus as Acts 2:42 shows us: "They [the first community] were faithful to the teaching of the apostles, the common life of sharing, the breaking of bread and the prayers."

Many Catholics gather to say formal and previously learned prayers (for example, the rosary or novenas) as a group. Other Catholics join together in Church venues or in each other's homes to practice spontaneous prayer and faith-sharing.

Sharing prayers with others can provide enriching benefits: (1) Listening to others pray or interpret Scripture can inspire, challenge, and teach us; (2) Praying out loud with others can sometimes make the experience more real; (3) Prayer groups can help overcome feelings of spiritual desolation and can provide informal spiritual direction.

Here is a format for shared prayer offered by Eamon Tobin, C.Ss.R., in his book *Prayer: A Handbook for Today's Catholic* (Liguori, MO: Liguori Publications, 1989):

- Begin with a song
- Spend a few minutes praising and thanking God for his goodness and blessings
- Spend time seeking God's mercy for our failings
- Read and share a Scripture text
- Take a few minutes to offer spontaneous prayer based on the text and reflections shared
- Spend some time sharing life experiences
- Conclude with some prayers of petition

Other group-prayer possibilities might include:

- Shared spiritual reading: Read a passage. Reflect silently. Then anyone who wishes may offer reactions or thoughts. Then observe another period of silence. Then form a spontaneous prayer in the form of direct address: "Father, we see from this reading...."

- Pick a certain topic, doctrine, or virtue and pool notions about what it means. Hear from each in turn with no pressure to participate.
- Plan prayer sessions around spiritual book reviews, encyclicals, or other study courses.
- Set up a free-flow prayer experience wherein everyone brings something to the meeting and shares it—a favorite prayer, reading, or recent experience. Discuss or pray about it as moved.

4. Prayer According to the Times of the Day

PRAYER THROUGH PARTICIPATION IN THE LITURGY OF THE HOURS

The Liturgy of the Hours is the prayer of the Church that sanctifies the hours of the day and night. It is a way of fulfilling the divine command to pray without ceasing. And it makes us more consciously aware that we are members of Christ's living Body. For monks and nuns whose very life is ordered around the Liturgy of the Hours, its full observance is practical. For lay people, a modified version is more suitable.

The essential components of the Liturgy of the Hours are hymns, psalms, readings from Scripture and the writings of the Fathers and Doctors of the Church, and prayer. If we buy the abbreviated liturgy of the Hours—a volume entitled *Christian Prayer* (Boston: Daughters of St. Paul, 1976)—it is all set out for us.

Here also is a simple outline of a brief Liturgy of the Hours that may be adapted for varying uses:

Morning Prayer
O Lord, open my lips…
And my tongue shall proclaim your praise.
Glory be to the Father and to the Son and to the Holy Spirit
as it was in the beginning, is now, and ever shall be. Amen.

Hymn

Psalms
Choose two or three psalms from the Book of Psalms in your Bible.
At the end of each psalm, say: *Glory be to the Father and to the Son and*
to the Holy Spirit as it was in the beginning, is now, and ever shall be.
Amen.

Reading
Read a passage from the Bible—from the Old Testament or the first
reading of the Mass of the day—and reflect on it.

Canticle of Zechariah (Luke 1:68–79)
Say the Canticle of Zechariah from the Bible, ending with a Glory Be.

Prayers of Intercession
Let us humbly and confidently bring our concerns to God.
For the Church…, let us pray to the Lord.
   Lord, hear our prayer.
For those serving in authority…, let us pray to the Lord.
   Lord, hear our prayer.
For our loved ones…, let us pray to the Lord.
   Lord, hear our prayer.
For our special needs…, let us pray to the Lord.
   Lord, hear our prayer.

For our departed…, let us pray to the Lord.
   Lord, hear our prayer.
Let us pray as our Lord has taught us. (Pray the Our Father.)

Concluding Prayer
God of infinite compassion and mercy, hear the prayer of your people. Bless this day, fill it with your peace and love. Make us sacraments of your love in the world. Grant this through Christ, our Lord. Amen.
Let us bless the Lord.
And give him thanks.

Evening Prayer
O God, come to my assistance.
O Lord, make haste to help me.
Glory be to the Father and to the Son, and to the Holy Spirit as it was in the beginning, is now, and ever shall be. Amen.

Hymn

Psalms
Choose two or three psalms from the Book of Psalms in the Bible.

Reading
Read a passage from the Bible, either from the Gospels or from the Gospel of today's Mass and reflect on it.

Canticle of Mary (Luke 1:46–55)
Pray the Canticle of Mary from the Bible. End with a Glory Be.

Prayers of Intercession
Let us humbly and confidently bring our concerns to God:
For the Church…, let us pray to the Lord.

Lord, hear our prayer.
For those serving in authority..., let us pray to the Lord.
  Lord, hear our prayer.
For our special needs..., let us pray to the Lord.
  Lord, hear our prayer.
For our departed..., let us pray to the Lord.
  Lord, hear our prayer.
Let us pray as our Lord has taught us (Pray the Our Father.)

Concluding Prayer
God of love, we thank you for the gift of this day with its many blessings. Forgive us for all the ways in which we have failed to use them well. Give us a peaceful night and the rest we need. Grant this through Christ, our Lord. Amen.
Let us bless the Lord.
And give him thanks.

PRAYERS UPON RISING AND RETIRING

These traditional times of prayer are the ones taught from childhood. It is important not to let these preset times fall into disuse. A famous book of prayers, *Private Devotions* by Lancelot Andrewes, gives a time-tested format for morning and evening prayers:

- Morning Prayers: (1) a prayer of awakening, especially requests peace for the world, repentance, and a good Christian death; (2) confession of sins; (3) commendation of the day to God.
- Evening Prayers: (1) a meditation of the day just past; (2) confession and request for forgiveness of sins committed during the day; (3) commendation of the night to God.
- A Seven-Day Cycle of Prayers for Each Day of the Week: (1) introduction; (2) confession; (3) prayer for grace; (4) profession; (5) intercession; (6) praise.

5. Prayer Using Specific Aids

PRAYING WITH OPEN EYES

This form of prayer is an act of mindfulness by which you choose an object—a leaf, a flowering bush, a rock, or even tools, a machine, or a building—paying attention to the smell, shape, and texture of things. This form of prayer asks you to enter into, to enjoy, to absorb, what is immediately before you. If done mindfully, an act of meditative prayer follows.

Next try to consider the possible symbolic associations of the object. For example, if one is observing a seedpod, an association to the parable of the sower would be appropriate. Pray then that the Holy Spirit will show you what you can learn from this mindful attention to a person or thing.

KEEPING A PRAYER JOURNAL

Some people find it a benefit to keep a journal of their moments in communion with God. Such a journal is not a diary but a way of expressing in your own written words your love for the Lord. It becomes a record of what you feel that the Holy Spirit is saying to you and what you are saying to God. The key to this effort is to write spontaneously just as the words and thoughts come to you.

Some others also find it helpful to record short passages from Scripture or from other spiritual writers, thus creating a very personal prayer book. Others still use a prayer journal to write "letters to God." Henri Nouwen's book, *A Cry for Mercy: Prayers From the Genesee*, is an example of such letter writing to God. In this book he also offers a "soul-teaching" on prayer.

To this journal, writers also add newspaper or magazine clippings, poetry of their own devising or by other authors, illustrations or other photos, and so on. But the most important warning here is not to become so self-absorbed in the technique that God is forgotten.

Some suggestions for writing in a prayer journal:

1. Come to a place of quiet, putting all outside distractions to rest.
2. Invite Jesus into your heart, always having faith that he knows what he wants to say to us and knows how to answer us back.
3. Use the prayer journal to keep in touch with your inner voices. Use this opportunity to get into honest touch with your feelings, good and bad, and bring them to Jesus.
4. Use the prayer journal to identify helps and hindrances to prayer, high and low points, and advancements and setbacks.

PRAYING WITH THE ROSARY

The rosary is truly a marverous combination of vocal and meditative prayer. The beads anchor our sense of touch, the mysteries provide focus for meditation, and the prayers give us a chance to repeat the greatest prayers of our tradition and the most fundamental expressions of our baptism into Christ. An explanation of the usual method of praying the rosary begins on page 134 of this book. How else could we use the rosary as part of our prayers? Here are some suggestions:

- Join a living rosary in which each bead is represented by a person who says that part of the prayer out loud.
- Walk the rosary: Combine the rosary with walking meditation.
- Pray the family rosary—even if only a single decade.
- Pray the psalms on the rosary.

- Pray the scriptural rosary—meditating on one single event for each of the five decades.
- As you meditate on each mystery of the rosary, place your-self in your mind within the scene taking place. For example, when the angel Gabriel appears to Mary at the Annuncia-tion, place yourself in the shadows and become a silent ob-server.

PRAYING WITH THE STATIONS OF THE CROSS

The Stations of the Cross are a series of fourteen scenes depicting Christ's passion, usually found on the interior walls of most churches. However, it is possible to pray with this devotional framework at any time or place by using books or pamphlets that show these fourteen stations.

The traditional Stations of the Cross, together with meditations adapted from the writings of John Cardinal Newman, appear on page 67. Pope John Paul II has given us a new way to pray the Stations of the Cross. He used a new series of fourteen stations on Good Friday in 1991; these are founded more closely on Scriptures: (1) Jesus Washes the Feet of His Disciples (Jn 13:2–5); (2) Jesus in the Garden (Mt 26:36–56); (3) Jesus Before the Jewish Authorities (Mt 26:57–75); (4) Jesus Before Pilate (Mt 27:1–26); (5) Jesus Is Scourged, Crowned, and Mocked (Mt 27:26–31); (6) Jesus Takes Up His Cross (Mk 15:20); (7) Simon Helps Jesus Carry His Cross (Mt 27:32); (8) Jesus Consoles the Women (Lk 23:27–31); (9) Jesus Is Nailed to the Cross (Mt 27:33–38); (10) "This Day You Will Be With Me in Paradise" (Lk 23:39–43); (11) "Behold Your Mother" (Jn 19:25–27); (12) Jesus Dies on the Cross (Mt 27:39–56); (13) The Burial of Jesus (Mt 27:57–66); (14) Jesus Rises (Mt 28:1–15).

Father Basil Pennington, in his book *Awake in the Spirit* (New York: Crossroad, 1992), gives the following method for praying the Way of the Cross:

There is in the Way of the Cross a very incarnational symbol. As we enter into this prayer, we actually walk with Christ. Our whole body enters into the prayer....We are conscious of walking with Christ, and that in the most sacred moments of his life....But this walking also symbolizes what we are doing and what we want as the fruit of the prayer. We are actually walking with Christ in our lives, sharing in his way of suffering that leads to death and life....

When we are to pray the Stations it is well to take a few minutes to prepare. We do not know how to pray as we ought but the Holy Spirit is within, to teach us and to pray with us. We might in imagination transport ourselves to Jerusalem with its Via Dolorosa. Or we might more personally just simply unite ourselves with Jesus and with Mary....

Once we are prepared, we walk to the first station. There is a moment of recognition of the event and then we enter into it in the way we have chosen for this particular journey to Calvary.

Some people like to genuflect or kneel for a moment when they come to each station and begin with the traditional prayer: "We adore you, O Christ, and we praise you because by your holy Cross you have redeemed the world."

Father Basil recommends choosing an allotted time for each station and, just before moving on, after our prayer of meditation or reflection, move to a more emotional prayer, speaking directly to our Lord or God the Father and kneeling for a bit before we leave each station.

PRAYING WITH SUNG PRAYER

Singing prayer is a form of vocal prayer. Listening to sung prayers such as the Taizé chants, hymns from John Michael Talbot, Gregorian chants, or the popular religious music of Robert and Robin Kochis (available through Liguori Publications) can be both prayer in itself and background for other types of resting in the presence of God.

Whether we listen to music or make music, individually or in a group, this experience can be a prayer opportunity. Hymns are often held in our memories long after spoken statements have faded. Hildegard of Bingen, eleventh-century mystic and musician, affirms the power of singing to bring us into relationship with God:

> The body is truly the garment of the soul, which has a living voice, for that reason it is fitting that the body simultaneously with the soul repeatedly sing praises to God through voice.
>
> HILDEGARD OF BINGEN

PRAYING WITH AN ICON

An icon is a sacred form of liturgical art that exclusively depicts images of Christ, the Mother of God, angels, saints, or events of sacred history. These images are often painted on garments, walls, panels, screens, and other portable surfaces. The Holy Spirit was regarded as working through the hands of the artists, who painted in a flat, two-dimensional, and very stylized manner, to avoid creating "graven images."

Sometimes icons are called windows to heaven and are venerated in the same way as holy Scripture. In fact, the Church teaches and affirms, in the words of the *Catechism of the Catholic Church,* that "Christian iconography expresses in images the same Gospel message that Scripture communicates by words. Image and word illuminate each other" (*CCC* §1160).

Eastern Catholic Churches connect icons to the life of Christ on earth, and the image created "without hands" is testimony to his Incarnation. Since icons are thought of as visible prayer, it is a helpful idea to spend time contemplating them, especially those from the Byzantine and Russian traditions. Some famous icons for possible meditation are Andrei Rublev's icon of the Blessed Trinity: "The Oak of Mamre," Christ the Vine, Our Lady of Vladimir, the Savior, and the Entombment. Small books containing full-color plates of icons, such as Iain Zaczek's *The Art of the Icon* (London: Studio Editions, 1994) can serve as prayer books.

To pray with an icon, you may wish to use these following steps. First, place yourself in the presence of God and fix your attention on the icon. Second, after studying the icon, think about its symbolism. Certain icons, such as Our Lady of Perpetual Help, have elaborate symbols. In this icon, the archangels Michael and Gabriel are carrying the instruments of the crucifixion, the gold background represents heaven, and the infant Jesus is looking away from his mother toward his mission in the world. Third, after lingering on the symbolic meaning, reflect on its implications for you. Some people feel the message so clearly that they say the icon "speaks" to them directly. Finally, accompany your ending meditative gaze into the picture with the Jesus Prayer or the Glory Be.

PRAYING WITH A CRUCIFIX

Spending time in communion with the Lord simply contemplating his image on the cross can be a fruitful way of deepening your awareness that "God so loved the world" that he gave the life of his son on the Cross. The Way of the Cross, with its fourteen stations, is a way of praying with a crucifix.

Saint Francis and the Franciscans also provide another cross on which to meditate: the San Damiano Cross, before which Saint Francis was praying when the Lord commissioned him in his service. This is an icon cross which includes various images on which to meditate: (1) Jesus, both wounded and strong, regal and suffering, is depicted; (2) Major witnesses: the Blessed Mother and the Beloved Disciple, Mary Magdalene, Mary (mother of James and wife of Cleopas), and the centurion of Mark's Gospel; (3) Minor Witnesses: Soldier who pierced Jesus' side is pictured as a smaller figure holding a spear and standing beneath the droplets of precious blood; opposite is the soldier who offered Jesus the vinegar-soaked sponges; (4) Six angels representing awe, discussion, and invitation; (5) Patron saints of Umbria (Italy); (6) Rooster representing Peter's denial; and (7) Jesus resurrected and ascended, being welcomed alive by ten angels and the power of God's right hand.

Meditation on artistic representations of the crucifixion of our Lord can be focused through paintings and etchings by Rembrandt, Fra Angelico, Tintoretto, El Greco, Georges Rouault, Marc Chagall, and many others.

PRAYING WITH A LABYRINTH

The labyrinth is an ancient spiritual tool that can guide us in prayer. A labyrinth is an intricate system of passageways, rooms, and doors, built so as to make finding the place of exit difficult. In medieval churches labyrinths were often traced out in mosaic patterns on the floors, or in paintings. The most famous labyrinth, dating from 1220 and forty-one feet wide, is found in the nave of Chartres Cathedral in France.

This labyrinth has been used by many for the purpose of prayerful devotion. Walking the labyrinth, either this one or others created specifically for the prayer experience, is a prayer form symbolizing our walk toward God. Some walk with a verbal prayer on their lips or in their hearts. Others hold a question or a petition and open themselves to hearing an answer or receiving an insight. Walking a labyrinth may be done individually or as a group.

PRAYING WITH THE JESUS PRAYER

The Jesus Prayer is another ancient prayer form that is regaining popularity in recent times. The traditional wording of the Jesus Prayer goes like this: "Lord Jesus, have mercy on me, a sinner." Some people shorten it to: "Jesus, have mercy on me"; and others simply say the word "Jesus."

This prayer has been used by Christians—especially Eastern Christians—since at least the fourth century. The Desert Fathers used the Jesus Prayer to implement our Lord's admonition to "pray without ceasing."

How, then, do we pray the Jesus Prayer? The nineteenth-century Russian author of *The Way of a Pilgrim* tells us how:

> Imagine your heart; direct your eyes as though you were looking at it through your breast, see the heart as vividly as you can, and listen attentively to its rhythmic beat. And when you have become accustomed to this, then begin to say the words of the prayer, while looking into your heart, to the rhythm of your heartbeat. With the first beat say "Lord," with the second "Jesus," with the third "Christ," and the with fourth "have mercy," and with the fifth "on me." And repeat this frequently....
>
> The next step, according to the writings of the Fathers, is to direct the flow of the Jesus Prayer in the heart in harmony with your breathing; that is, while inhaling say, "Lord Jesus Christ," and while exhaling say, "have mercy on me." Practice this as often as possible, gradually increasing the time, and before too long you will experience a kind of pleasant pain in the heart, a warmth, and a sense of burning. Thus, with the help of God, you will attain self-activating prayer of the heart.

This prayer is also known as the Prayer of the Heart. As its practice has become more widespread, some have changed the wording of the prayer to suit their own needs: "Gracious God, give me peace"; "Jesus, my brother, heal me"; or "Holy Spirit, console me."

6. Praying With the Body

THE PRAYER OF BREATH

The Breath Prayer is really a form of the Jesus Prayer. Here is Jane E. Vennard's instructions for this prayer in her book *Praying With Body and Soul* (Minneapolis: Augsburg, 1999):

When you are ready, take a few deep breaths and attend gently to both the inhalation and the exhalation. Place one hand near your nose so you can feel the breath going in and out....Place your other hand on your chest so you can feel the gentle rise and fall of your lungs....Gradually begin to imagine that each breath moves beyond your lungs into your entire body. Follow your breath down into your belly...into your legs...all the way to your toes....Imagine your breath filling your shoulders... flowing down your arms and into your hands and fingertips.... Imagine your breath soothing and easing your neck... circulating through your brain...massaging the space behind your eyes.

As you feel your breath in every part of your being, breath a prayer of thanksgiving for the breath of life....Be aware of the abundance of air...the ease with which it flows...and how little thought you have to give to this life-giving gift. Discover a phrase you can pray to the rhythm of your breathing, such as, "The breath of the Holy Spirit; I give thanks." Stay with your breathing and praying as long as you wish....Then close your prayer in any way that seems appropriate.

PRAYER POSTURE

The posture of prayer contributes much to its quality; efforts should be made to find a body position that promotes stillness of body and calmness of mind that allows us to remain calm and alert. Abbot

Michael Casey in his book *Toward God: The Ancient Wisdom of Western Prayer* (Liguori, MO: Liguori Publications, 1996) gives some sound advice:

> The paramount element of good posture [in prayer] is keeping the spine straight. To slump or slouch is not only externally ugly, but seems to interfere with one's inner sense of being physically together, or doing something and not just letting time pass. Whether one sits or kneels or uses a prayer stool makes no great difference, so long as one's back is straight— not in a military way, but in a calm natural way....
>
> Posture is an expression of our prayer. In its own body language, the physical organism unites with the heart in turning toward God. By keeping still, we renounce busyness. By unity and directedness of posture, we express determination to unite all our powers in seeking God. By being on the floor, we signal putting aside our executive self-image, simply conscious of being before God in utter humility.

Glossary of Significant Terms Relating to Prayer and Praying

Abba (ah-bah)   A word from the Aramaic language meaning "Father." *Abba* was used by Jesus when, in great agony, he prayed in the garden that his hour of suffering might pass from him (Mk 14:36). The use of this word—originally spoken only within the family as a term of great respect, love, and intimacy—puts Christ's status as Son of God on an almost familiar basis and expresses his confidence in his almighty Father.

In Galatians 4:6 and Romans 8:15, Paul records that the early Christian community used "*Abba*, Father" as a cry spoken by those who have been spiritually adopted as sons of God. Because those who are baptized also are sons and daughters who have received the Spirit of God's Son, they also are privileged to say *Abba* and model their own prayer life after that of Jesus'. They too can pray to the Father in this most intimate way, asking for help and the ability to discern the Father's will.

adoration   Conscious act of prayer by which God alone is recognized and praised as worthy of supreme worship. Adoration is essentially an act of body, mind, and will, but it is expressed and accomplished in external acts of sacrifice, prayer, reverence, and humility. Adoration is identified with the word *latria* meaning worship intended for God alone (in contrast to *dulia*, that worship accorded the angels and saints).

Before the Second Vatican Council (1962–1965), adoration was almost entirely associated with the Eucharist and, by extension, Forty Hours Devotion and Benediction of the Blessed Sacrament.

affective prayer   Prayer that comes from the heart and evokes the emotions and feelings in expressions of loving devotion to God. Affective prayer involves the whole person and may be contrasted with dutiful or formulaic prayer that may involve only the mind.

Some examples of affective prayer are the Psalms from the Bible which express powerful feelings of friendship and love for God, the pouring out of the heart as practiced by Saint Alphonsus Liguori, or even the quiet stirring of the spirit as it reaches out in praise and joy to experience the presence of God.

Amen   Word used at the end of prayers or at certain points in the Mass to indicate agreement and conclusion. *Amen* is a Hebrew word meaning "so be it," and is used by the Israelites in the Old Testament to signify their acceptance of God's commands.

In the New Testament Gospels, it is said twice in order to emphasize the importance of the words that follow ("Amen, Amen, I say to you"). In the epistles, *Amen* is used as an exclamation of faith in God's promises and Christ's final victory over sin.

The *Amen* response is an important affirmation of the people throughout the celebration of the Mass. It is said at the end of the Opening Prayer, the Prayer Over the Gifts, and the Prayer After Communion. The people also say or sing what is often referred to as the "Great Amen" at the end of the Eucharistic Prayer. They also respond with *Amen* at the point of receiving the body and blood of Christ at Communion.

Angelus   Prayer comprised of four short sentences that are said by the officiator followed by four responses interspersed with Hail Marys and concluding with a petition for God's grace through the Incarnation. Its name comes from the opening words in Latin of the first sentence: *Angelus Domini* ("Angel of the Lord").

Today, this prayer is said morning, noon, and evening and accompanied by the tolling of bells. Following the custom of his predecessors, Pope John Paul II recites the *Angelus* every Sunday from a window of the Apostolic Palace and concludes this recitation with his blessing.

Historically, the *Angelus* is associated with peace as when Pope Callistus III ordered the daily ringing of the bells at midday with the praying of three Hail Marys for the success of the Crusades. Finally, Pope Benedict XIV stipulated that the *Angelus* be replaced by the Marian antiphon *Regina Caeli* during Easter time.

A certain order is followed for the ringing of the bells: they are tolled three times at each invocation and end with nine strokes for the recitation of the final prayer. It is customary for those saying the *Angelus* to kneel with the exception of Sundays and holy days, when it is prayed standing accompanied by a genuflection at the third sentence.

Ave Maria (ah-veh mah-ree'-ah)   Term for the Hail Mary taken from the first two words of the Latin version of the prayer and which draws its origins from the greeting of the archangel Gabriel to the Blessed Virgin Mary at the Annunciation as recorded in the Gospel of Luke. See **Hail Mary.**

Benedicite (bay'-nay-dee'-chee-tay)   Word meaning "bless" which comes from the first words of the Latin version of the Canticle of the Three Young Men (Dan 3:19–30). This song of praise is sung by Shadrach, Meshach, and Abednego when they survived King Nebuchadnezzar's fiery furnace into which they had been thrown. The three young men were companions of the prophet Daniel and were ordered into the furnace for refusing to serve false gods. This canticle is recited or sung on some Sundays during the Liturgy of the Hours, and also on feasts and solemnities.

Benediction of the Blessed Sacrament   Ceremony in which a consecrated host is exposed (in a gold container called a *monstrance* or in a covered chalice similar to a *ciborium*) on an altar and venerated by those present. The service includes readings of the Word of God, songs, a period of silent prayer, and a blessing of the congregation with the host.

The practice of Benediction dates back to the Middle Ages when people felt a desire to see the holy Eucharist, especially since personal reception of the Blessed Sacrament occurred infrequently. The popularity of Benediction was furthered by the celebrations surrounding the feast of Corpus Christi, including the exposition of the host and processions.

The celebration of Benediction and the exposition of the Blessed Sacrament declined after Vatican II (1962–1965), since the ceremony had come to be regarded by some of the faithful as a substitute for the Mass. However, in 1973, the Vatican reaffirmed the importance of the exposition of the Eucharist as a way of enhancing the prayer life of the people.

Benedictional   Book containing a collection of blessings that originated in Western Europe and England during the Middle Ages. In the United States, the present *De Benedictionibus* is published in English as the *Book of Blessings*.

Benedictus **(bay-nay-dik'-tus)**   Latin title of the Canticle of Zechariah as recorded in the Gospel of Luke (1:68–79) taken from its first word, "Blessed be the Lord God of Israel" (*Benedictus Dominus Deus Israel*). The Canticle of Zechariah is a song of praise sung by the father of John the Baptist at the circumcision of his son. The Church sings or recites this canticle as a part of the Liturgy of the Hours.

blessing   Prayer asking for God's gifts and the sanctification of various groups, individuals, or objects. The ceremony of blessing usually involves the naming of the person, group, or object, and the raising of the right hand in the Sign of the Cross. Blessings are sacramentals derived from our priesthood of baptism. Thus, every baptized person is summoned to be a "blessing" and also to bless. For this reason, lay people may direct certain rites of blessings while others are reserved to those who are ordained (*CCC* §§1669, 1671).

Blessings, Book of   English name of that part of the Roman ritual containing the official rites for the blessings of persons, places, and things in formats revised according to the liturgical principles handed down by Vatican II. Part I of the *Book of Blessings* contains blessings for families (married couples, parents, adoptive children, and so on). Also included are blessings for the sick and prayers for those who suffer from addiction, abuse, or who are victims of crimes. Other blessings in Part I focus on religious meetings of various types, travelers, and pilgrims.

Part II contains blessings for varying types of activities, buildings, and blessings before and after meals. Blessings for items used in public and private prayer are contained in parts III and IV, while parts V and

VI present blessings related to parish ministers (servers, musicians, and so on) and other parish-level occasions.

The revised rites of blessings are marked by these characteristics: a formal greeting based on words from Scripture and related to the occasion; a choice of readings from Scripture that are to be read before the blessing occurs; series of intercessory prayers for use with longer rites of blessing; a concluding rite of blessing and dismissal which is related to scriptural themes.

breviary (bree'-vee-air-ee) Term used previously for the book containing the Church's daily public prayer, now called the Liturgy of the Hours and formerly termed the Divine Office (a name sometimes still popularly used).

In the Middle Ages, the full form of the Church's public prayer was chanted in monasteries and cathedrals; thus it required many books: a book of antiphons (antiphonary), a book of psalms (psalter), a book of readings or lessons, a book of martyrs (martyrology), and a book of hymns. To assist those who traveled and who could not have been expected to carry such a number of books with them, the principal parts of the of the prayers were organized into a shortened format and so the book containing this text was called a *breviarium*, or an "abridgment."

The entire cycle of the Church's official public prayer as commonly used in the United States is contained in a four-volume English translation titled *Liturgy of the Hours*, and a shorter abridgement is contained in a one-volume book entitled *Christian Prayer*.

Canon of the Mass Former name of the main part of the Mass, which is now referred to as the Eucharistic Prayer. The word "canon" derives from the Greek and means "rule" in the sense of an established standard. The Canon of the Mass refers to the single Eucharistic Prayer that was prescribed in the Western Church from the Middle Ages until the change to new eucharistic prayers after Vatican II.

canticle (kan'-tuh-cal)   Poetic passage from the Bible often used as part of the liturgy, especially the Liturgy of the Hours. Canticles from the Old Testament include the Canticle of Moses (Ex 15:1–13, 17–18), the Canticle of Hannah (1 Sam 2:1–10), the Canticle of Judith (Jdt 16:2–17), and the Canticle of Isaiah (Is 45:9–19). Canticles in the New Testaments include the Canticle of Mary (Lk 1:46–55) and the Canticle of Zechariah (Lk 1:68–79).

Catholic Household Blessings and Prayers   Companion to the *Book of Blessings* devised by the bishops of the United States and containing prayers and blessings for use by families and individuals in the home as part of the daily prayer of every Catholic. The first part of this volume contains prayers to observe the activities of the day: for rising, to bless the day's work, blessings before and after meals, and at retiring. Part II gives prayers and blessings arranged according to the liturgical season, for example, blessings for the Advent wreath, for Easter, and even national days of observance. In part III, blessings and prayers that cover the life cycle of the family from childhood through sickness and death are presented. Part IV gives blessings for specific places, times, and objects, while part V is a compilation of prayers, including the traditional litanies, eucharistic and Marian devotions, and a simplified form of the Morning and Evening Prayer of the Liturgy of the Hours.

centering prayer   Method of prayer that is a gateway to contemplation and which focuses on a loving concentration on God. It is based on the practices of the Desert Fathers and the teaching contained in *The Cloud of Unknowing*. It is a form of prayer that leads to contemplation. At one stage prayer can be thought of as ideas or emotions directed toward God and expressed in words. Centering prayer aims to develop a spirit of contemplation in which a person abides in the quiet of God and lays aside all words.

Cistercian Father Basil Pennington describes centering prayer as "going beyond thought and image, beyond the senses of the rational mind, to the center of our being where God is working wonderful work. There God our Father is not only bringing us forth at each moment in his wonderful creative love, but by virtue of filiation, which we received at baptism, he is indeed making us sons and daughters, one with his own Son...."

Another teacher of centering prayer, Father Thomas Keating, outlines the method of centering prayer as follows: (1) Choose a sacred word as the sign of your intent to open your awareness to God; (2) Sit in a comfortable position with eyes closed, and quietly introduce this sacred word into your mind; (3) When you feel grounded in God's presence, drop the word and wait in silence. When you become aware of thoughts, return quietly to the sacred word and from there, back to the wordless state of blankness; (4) Keep all sense perceptions, feelings, images, memories, and self-talk away during this period of centering prayer; (5) At the end of the prayer period, remain in silence with eyes closed for a few minutes to give yourself a brief space to readjust to the external world.

Centering prayer is not an end in itself, but a way to open ourselves to God and to bring God into union with us. Centering prayer is usually done regularly, sometimes twice a day for a period of twenty minutes or so.

Collect   Former name for the opening prayer of the holy Mass, now called in English the Opening Prayer. The name "collect" arose from the concept of the priest collecting the prayers of the faithful and offering them to God in the name of those assembled. The Opening Prayer takes place at the end of the introductory rites of the Mass, prior to the beginning of the Liturgy of the Word. The Opening Prayer is usually addressed to the First Person of the Holy Trinity and ends, as do all liturgical prayers, with a concluding part in honor of the Son in unity with the Holy Spirit (*CCC* §§1346, 1348).

Compline (kom'-pline)   Concluding night office of the Liturgy of the Hours. It means "to complete" and marks the end of the day. It follows the office of Vespers, or evening prayer. The present night office is made up of these elements: an examination of conscience, a hymn or psalm that varies with the liturgical season, a short lesson, a response, and the Canticle of Simeon. Before the revisions of Vatican II, the office of Compline chiefly consisted of a brief lesson, the *Confiteor*, three psalms and a response, a hymn, a canticle, and an antiphon in honor of Mary.

Confiteor (kahn-fee'-tay-ohr)   Word meaning "I confess" and used as the title and first Latin word of a prayer which is an optional part of the introductory ceremonies at the holy sacrifice of the Mass in the Roman rite. The *Confiteor* is a confession of sins and prayer for forgiveness which was once said by the priest at the front of the altar before beginning Mass. The *Confiteor* grew out of the custom in the Middle Ages of the clergy saying prayers of unworthiness during the procession to the altar.

Creed, Athanasian   One of the authorized statements of the truths of faith, originating in the fourth or fifth century and attributed to Saint Athanasius. It deals primarily with the two doctrines of the Trinity and the Incarnation which this creed states and restates in various ways. It also gives the penalties to be levied on those who refuse to accept the dogmas articulated in this creed.

creeds   Summaries of the principle truths of the Church written as professions of belief. Creeds are basically prayers of faith. The Catholic Church possesses many kinds of creeds, including the "rules of faith" fashioned by Irenaeus and Tertullian, the Old Roman Creed, and the "ecumenical creeds," such as the Apostles' Creed, the Nicene Creed, the Athanasian Creed, and the Creed of the Third Council of Constantinople.

Creeds function in a variety of ways in the liturgy, as a common confession of faith, as a declaration at baptism, and as private prayer (*CCC* §185–197).

contemplation   Type of prayer in which the mind and the will give way to a wordless concentration on God, an awareness of his presence, a knowledge of his works, and a loving union with him. Contemplation is considered the highest form of prayer and is traditionally set apart from meditation. Such distinctions arise from the efforts of medieval writers to isolate four stages of the contemplative process: (1) Reading of the Scriptures and reflection on the Word of God, known as *lectio divina*; (2) repetition of a word or phrase until the mind and heart are completely taken over by it; (3) the transition to prayer as conversation with God; and, finally, (4) the emergence of a contemplative state of pure presence in God.

In practice, contemplation takes different forms and has been defined differently by different writers. Those who have written on this subject include Origen (c. 185–255), Gregory of Nyssa (c. 335–395), the fourteenth-century anonymous author of *The Cloud of Unknowing*, Meister Eckhart (1260–1327), Teresa of Ávila (1515–1582), and John of the Cross (1542–1591).

Day Hours   All the hours (specific intervals of the daily cycle of the Church's prayer) of the Divine Office except Matins. Prior to Vatican II (1962–1965), some books were published in English that contained all the hours of the Divine Office except Matins (celebrated around midnight) which had included a long set of psalms and readings. These books were called in English, for example, *Day Hours of the Roman Breviary*. Since the revisions of Vatican II, "day hours" probably more properly refers to what is now called Daytime Prayer, which is comprised of the three lesser hours, only one of which need be said by clergy and religious in active life: midmorning (Terce, or the "third" hour, prayed about 9:00 A.M.), midday (Sext, or the "sixth" hour, prayed about noon), and midafternoon (None, or the "ninth" hour, prayed about 3:00 P.M.).

day of recollection   Day spent as part of a group gathered together to quietly reflect or to collect one's thoughts in order to progress in spiritual understanding. Days of recollection can include special prayers, conferences, and discussion groups. They differ from retreats in that they are shorter in length and have no overnight accomodation requirements. Thus, the specialized services of a retreat center are not necessary.

days of prayer   Days of individual and communal prayer designated by the local bishop of a diocese in which all Catholics are asked to pray for special needs and concerns. Types of topics include prayers of thanksgiving to God, human rights, forgiveness of sins, or peace. These locally determined days of prayer are widely valued and perhaps arose out of the ancient Christian traditions of ember days and rogation days. In the third century, seasonal days of prayer and fasting four times a year came to be known as "ember days." During the fifth century in France, certain days were set aside by Church authorities to pray for protection against evil and damage to crops. These came to be known as "rogation days." Later, fixed dates for these observances were set for the worldwide Church community.

decade   Group or division of ten. In the Roman Catholic sense, a decade is a section of the Rosary of Our Lady made up of one Our Father, ten Hail Marys, and one Glory Be. These prayers are said while meditating on one of the fifteen mysteries of the rosary.

devotions   Optional practices, usually involving prayer or reflection, that are cause for worship or service of God. Devotions are usually distinguished from formal liturgical prayer, such as the holy sacrifice of the Mass. They can be seen as a form of popular expression of religion that creates a bridge between an intellectual understanding of the faith and the observance of that faith in ordinary life. Pilgrimages, the rosary, novenas, and devotions to the Sacred Heart are all forms of popular devotions.

Though properly formatted devotions that lead back to a more committed gospel life and to the Mass are reaffirmed by Vatican II, popular devotions should always be in harmony with the worship of the Church.

Divine Office   Name formerly used (and still used in some contexts) to designate the official public prayer of the Church. Since these intervals of prayer are designed to sanctify the hours of the day, the Vatican II revision of these sets of prayer are called the "Liturgy of the Hours." It is worth noting that the title page of the official English-language book containing the forms and prayers for the Liturgy of the Hours still bears the name "The Divine Office," appearing above the title *The Liturgy of the Hours of the Roman Rite*. See **Liturgy of the Hours, Day Hours, Breviary.**

Divine Praises   Series of acclamations blessing God, Jesus Christ, the Blessed Virgin, and Saint Joseph. The Divine Praises, familiar to many as an optional part of the reposing of the Blessed Sacrament, were attributed to Luigi Felici, an eighteenth-century Jesuit, who composed them as reparation for blasphemy and profanity. Over the years, various phrases were added and indulgences attached.

eucharistic adoration   Devotional practices focused on Christ's presence as Lord and Savior in the consecrated bread and wine. These devotions include exposition of the Blessed Sacrament usually followed by Benediction, eucharistic processions, visits to the Blessed Sacrament, and holy hours of adoration.

Public or private devotions to the Eucharist were inspired by the desire of the thirteenth-century faithful to look at the consecrated host in order to achieve interior communion with Christ. These outside-the-Mass devotions became popular almost to the point of becoming as important as the celebration of the Mass, sometimes replacing it in the minds of the ordinary Catholics.

After Vatican II (1962–1965), these eucharistic experiences were seen as an extension of the Eucharistic Liturgy itself which is the summit of Christian Life. Thus, they provide people with additional time to contemplate and revere the mysteries celebrated in the Eucharist and to seek from Christ strength for the journey of discipleship.

extraliturgical services   Forms of public worship, such as the Stations of the Cross, Forty Hours Devotion, or the rosary, which may make use of liturgical components (for example, Scripture readings), but which are not part of the Church's official worship. Though these practices are often celebrated in parishes and play a healthy part in Christian life, they must be in balance with the Church's liturgy.

Forty Hours Devotion   Traditional type of worship consisting of a period of prayer before the Blessed Sacrament in honor of the real presence of Jesus Christ in the Eucharist. A common order of Forty Hours Devotion begins with a celebration of the Mass, followed by the placement of a consecrated host in a large receptacle which is then carried through the church in procession. The Eucharist is then placed on the main church altar for all to visit during the next forty hours or so. The forty-hour period ends with the recital of certain prayers, the singing of appropriate hymns and a celebration of the Mass in which the Eucharist is reposed back in the tabernacle.

The present form of Forty Hours Devotion grew out a diverse set of practices that finally coalesced in Milan, Italy, in the mid-sixteenth century. Early observances of Forty Hours (said to commemorate the time Our Lord spent in the tomb) were characterized by penitence, reparation for excesses, and divine protection from various calamities. From Italy, Forty Hours Devotion spread to other parts of the world.

Present ceremonies concentrate on devotion to Jesus in the Eucharist rather than penance and reparation. Forty Hours Devotion was promoted in the United States by Saint John Neumann, the bishop of Philadelphia, and encouraged a sense of parish community. By 1973, the Church recommended the exposition of the Blessed Sacrament in each parish for an extended period of time for each year. These decrees remind us that these eucharistic devotions should always be secondary in importance to the celebration of the Mass.

Francis, Prayer of   One of the most popular of Christian prayers also known as the Peace Prayer of Saint Francis. This prayer is attributed to Saint Francis of Assisi, but was probably not written by him. Here is the text:

> Lord, make me an instrument of your peace;
> where there is hatred, let me sow love;

where there is injury, pardon;
where there is doubt, faith;
where there is despair, hope;
where there is darkness, light;
and where there is sadness, joy;
Grant that I may not so much seek
 to be consoled as to console;
to be understood as to understand;
to be loved as to love;
for it is in giving that we receive;
it is in pardoning that we are pardoned;
and it is in dying that we are born to eternal life.

genuflection Practice of bending the right knee to the floor, or sometimes the touching of both knees to the ground, and bowing the head as an act of prayerful adoration. Genuflection originated in courtly ceremonials and later was extended as a means of honoring the Cross, the altar, and the Blessed Sacrament. In the Eucharistic Liturgy, the presider genuflects after the elevation of the host and chalice and before Communion.

grace at meals Brief prayers asking a blessing on the food to be eaten at a meal, a desire that Christ will be present in the sharing of the food, and an offering of thanksgiving after the meal is finished. These prayers are generally very simple and can follow a prescribed form or be spontaneous.

Hail Mary Popular prayer based on two texts from Luke: the angel's greeting spoken to the Virgin Mary at the Annunciation (Lk 1:28), and on Elizabeth's greeting when Mary visits her (Lk 1:42). This prayer is also called the Angelic Salutation. The Hail Mary was widely said by the thirteenth century when directives from the bishops of Paris expressed the wish that the faithful should learn the Hail Mary, in addition to the Our Father and the Creed. Though the Hail Mary is not used in the Mass, it is included in the Little Office of the Blessed Virgin Mary and many devotions, most notably the rosary.

271

Hesychasm (hes-i-kasm)   Method of prayer of the heart characterized by devotion to the name of Jesus (usually through one particular prayer: Lord Jesus Christ, have mercy on me); constant repetition of the name of Jesus; a deep sense of sorrow for sin; and the use of these character-istics to achieve a contemplative sense of inner stillness. Sometimes this method of prayer was supported by exercises: regulated breathing and a posture of bowed head, chin on chest, and eyes fixed on the place of the heart. Hesychasm is part of the prayer tradition of Eastern Christianity passed down for many centuries. It was described by Symeon the New Theologian (d. 1022) and by Gregory of Palamas (d. 1359) and was reborn in popularity with the publication of spiritual texts called the *Philokalia* which was edited by Nicodemus of the Holy Mountain (d. 1809) and Macarius of Corinth (d. 1805). It is through the *Philokalia* and the Russian *The Way of a Pilgrim* that this tradition came to influence Western spirituality.

holy hour   Devotion that involves an uninterrupted hour of prayer and meditation in the presence of the Blessed Sacrament, either exposed on the altar or reposed in the tabernacle. The custom of making a holy hour is said to derive from the query of Jesus to his apostle Peter: "Could you not watch with me one hour?" (Mt 26:40) and practiced further by Saint Margaret Mary Alocoque who kept a holy hour in response to a message from Christ who promised her a share in his agony in Gethsemani. Holy hours can include time for meditation on the Pas-sion of Our Lord, adoration of Jesus Christ really present in the Eucha-rist, silent reflection, meditation on Scripture, reading of a spiritual book, praying silently. Communal observances may include a homily, Benediction of the Blessed Sacrament, and shared prayer.

holy water   Water that has been blessed for religious purposes and which thus becomes a sacramental used by the faithful to ask for God's blessing either on people or objects. The symbolism of water as pure and life-giving recalls our baptism, and it is for this reason that fonts containing blessed water are placed near the entrances to churches.

Hours, Book of   Devotional books used primarily by lay people during the Middle Ages as a substitute for participation in the common prayer of the Church because they did not know Latin or because they lived too far away from a place where the hours were observed. Books of Hours, containing popular devotions to be said at the canonical hours of the day, were often commissioned by wealthy people and were usually works of art in and of themselves. These books were greatly prized and were handed down from generation to generation.

indulgences   Remission before God of the temporal punishment due to sins as a result of certain prayers or good works. It is important to note in this explanation that indulgences do not remit the sins themselves nor do they remit eternal punishment. They, as granted by God through the Church, only remit the temporal aspects of sin. The Church strictly governs the use of indulgences and publishes official lists of the prayers and good works to which indulgences are attached.

intercession   Prayer offered for other persons and their needs. Membership in the Body of Christ through baptism which creates a bond that unites the whole Church makes us capable of this kind of prayer and demands that we perform this act for others out of our love for them. The chief intercessors on our behalf are Jesus Christ, his mother Mary, and the saints.

Intercessory prayer is also a form of liturgical and private prayer. Prayers of intercession are said on behalf of the pope, the bishops, the clergy, and the people of God during the Eucharistic Prayer of the Mass. Scriptures abound with the use of intercessory prayer on the part of Moses, Abraham, and the prophets, kings, and priests. In the New Testament, Jesus' own prayer shows his ultimate desire to ask his Father to take care of the needs of the faithful.

Kyrie eleison (kee'-ree-ay ay-lay'-ee-son)   Greek words meaning "Lord, have mercy," which were used together with *Christe eleison* meaning "Christ, have mercy" as a litany-like chant in honor of the Holy Trinity which served as an introduction to the priest's opening prayer during the Mass. At this time, the words, in the vernacular, are part of the penitential rite of the holy Mass.

Lauds   Traditional name for the Morning Prayer of the Liturgy of the Hours, the morning parallel to Vespers, or the Evening Prayer. Lauds and Vespers are the chief, or hinge, hours of the Liturgy of the Hours. Elements of Lauds include an invitatory verse and Psalm 95 (several other psalms are given as options) if it is the first office of the day; if the Office of Readings (passages of Scripture for sacred reading together with extracts from spiritual writers) precedes Lauds immediately, Lauds begins simply with the morning hymn; two psalms with their antiphons; an Old Testament canticle, a short Scripture reading which varies with the day, the season, and the feast and responsory; the Canticle of Zechariah; intercessions; the Lord's Prayer; the concluding prayer; and the dismissal.

lectio divina **(lek-see-oh duh-vee'-nah)**   Holy reading of sacred Scripture or the Fathers of the Church along with spiritual reflection undertaken as a pathway to prayer. Long associated with monastic practice, for example, the Rule of Saint Benedict assigned this type of meditative reading for as long as two to three hours daily, *lectio divina* is now receiving fuller attention among all the baptized as a means of enriching one's prayer and spiritual life.

Leonine Prayers   Prayers once recited by priests and people after Mass by order of Pope Leo XIII. The prayers consisted of three Hail Marys, the Hail, Holy Queen, a versicle and response, a prayer for the conversion of sinners and the exaltation of the Church, a prayer to Saint Michael the archangel and a brief ejaculation in honor of the Sacred Heart. Originally these prayers were offered for relief from the situation imposed on the Church by the loss of the Papal States, and then for the conversion of Russia. The custom of reciting these prayers after Mass came to an end in 1964.

litany   Form of prayer focusing on a group of invocations to which the people respond, for example, with the words "pray for us" or "deliver us from evil." In their early development, litanies were petitions repeated over and over again. During the Middle Ages, litanies were included as part of church rituals such as Benediction and the Forty Hours Devotion. One of the oldest of these prayer forms is the Litany of Saints, and gradually other litanies arose in honor of Mary, the Mother of Jesus.

Today litanies are used as part of the Church's worship (for example, the Litany of the Saints is recited at the Easter Vigil and at ordination ceremonies) and as part of private prayer. Of the litanies that have developed only a few are now approved for use in public worship: Litany of the Saints, Litany of the Blessed Virgin Mary, Litany of the Crowning of a Statue of the Blessed Virgin, Litany of the Sacred Heart, Litany of the Precious Blood, and the Litany of Saint Joseph.

Litany of the Saints   Prayer invoking a series of saints read by a leader, to which the people respond "pray for us." In the second part of the litany, the leader makes a series of petitions addressed to Christ and appropriate responses are made by the congregation. This list of saints was lengthy and was not uniform until Pope Pius V. The revision of the litany in 1969 provides both a long and a short version of the litany and also allows for variations both in the list of the saints and in the petitions according to the occasion.

Little Office of the Blessed Virgin Mary   Abridged version of the common office of the Blessed Virgin Mary that may have originated as early as the ninth century in conjunction with a Saturday Mass in honor of Mary composed by Alcuin (d. 804). This Little Office consists of hymns, antiphons, psalms, and other prayers arranged according to a daily cycle of prayer as found in the Divine Office (now the Liturgy of the Hours). Some communities of monks added the Little Office to their daily prayer, others used it as a special Saturday devotion; and some communities of women took this Little Office as their standard daily prayer.

Even with the tendency for many people who would have used the Little Office in the past to now use the official Liturgy of the Hours, a new and expanded version of the Little Office was published for those who are not bound to recite the Liturgy of the Hours. It should be noted that the revised Liturgy of the Hours provides for a Saturday memorial of the Blessed Virgin Mary during Ordinary Time, and the texts for this Saturday Office are taken almost entirely from the former Little Office.

Liturgy of the Hours   Official daily prayer of the Church whose aim is to praise God and dedicate all the elements of daily life to the service of sanctification. As used here, the term "hours" means certain set intervals of prayer which occur periodically around the clock.

Members of the early Church gathered to pray daily—morning, noon, and night. These popular prayer services were later taken up by those who lived in monasteries where the community gathered to pray, sometimes as often as seven times a day. As this "Divine Office" became more complex and regulated, the participation of the laity ceased, and the canonical hours became the exclusive province of clergy and religious.

The Second Vatican Council (1962–1965) reformed the Church's Liturgy of the Hours, "so that it could more fittingly be used by the clergy and other members of the Church in the circumstances of modern life." The council made these changes: (1) Lauds (Morning Prayer) and Vespers (Evening Prayer) are the "two hinges on which the daily Office turns" and are seen as the chief hours of prayer; (2) Compline (Night Prayer) is the mark of the end of the day and is to be said before retiring, even if this is after midnight; (3) Matins, renamed Office of Readings, became the "floating" hour and may be said at any time of the day; (4) The Hour of Prime (which was originally the first hour said about 6:00 A.M.) was discontinued because of its duplication by Lauds; (5) Daytime Prayer (made up of the three minor hours of Terce, Sext, and None) need be said only once.

In the United States the official edition is published in four volumes and entitled the *Liturgy of the Hours*. In England and Ireland, a three-volume edition is called *The Divine Office*. One-volume shorter versions, usually containing Morning, Evening, and Night Prayer along with a selection from Midday Prayer and the Office of Readings, are available and entitled *Christian Prayer*. Shorter abridgments, such as *Shorter Morning and Evening Prayer* and *Shorter Christian Prayer*, have also been published.

Lord's Prayer   Also called the "Our Father" and the *Pater Noster*. The Lord's Prayer is so titled because it is the prayer that Jesus gave to his disciples as the model of all Christian prayer. Two versions of the Lord's Prayer are given in the Gospels: In Matthew 6:9–15 in the middle of the Sermon on the Mount; and in Luke 11:2–4 as a response to the disciples request to "teach us to pray."

This most basic prayer of Christianity (the *Didache* of the first century stipulates that it be prayed three times a day) is created in a simple framework: homage to God and petitions of needs (forgiveness of sins, deliverance from temptation, daily sustenance). The Our Father is such a perfect prayer that it is offered every time the Eucharistic Liturgy is celebrated at the beginning of the Communion Rite, where the priest and people pray together "in the words our Savior gave us."

The Our Father is also an important part of the rosary and other forms of devotion.

Kiss of Peace   Gesture affirming an attitude of inner peace which was used by early Christians as a seal of the prayer which precedes it in the Mass.

***Magnificat* (mahg-ni'-fee-kaht)**   Canticle of Mary found in Luke 1:46–55 and spoken in response to her cousin Elizabeth on the occasion of Mary's visit to her. This hymn is a song of praise to God for all he had done for her, a vindication of the "lowly," and thanksgiving for the mercy he has shown Israel. The model of Mary's canticle is that of Hannah's hymn of praise (1 Sam 2:1–10) in the Old Testament and another prayer by a woman to whom God has shown great favor.

meditation   Form of mental prayer and reflection on God or a scriptural or religious idea that leads to an elevation of the soul and to spiritual transformation and enlightenment. Meditation differs from mere thinking about spiritual matters because it is a form of prayer. Meditation differs from vocal prayer because it is almost exclusively an interior action. Meditation is sometimes distinguished from contemplation and seen as a preparation for it—meditation resting on the use of words while contemplation is an imageless and thought-free act of being with God rather than talking to him or thinking about him. Contemplation is pure prayer, while meditation makes use of the mind, the emotions, and memory in a quest for God.

The method of Christian meditation has been developed more deeply through the work of John Main, a Benedictine monk, who has fostered the establishment of worldwide meditation groups that encourage regular daily practice. An aspect of Main's meditation method is the repetition of a Christian word in order to find true peace, a calmness of soul, and diminishment of the consciousness of self in favor of an awareness of Christ.

Memento   Word referring to those times in the Eucharistic Prayers of the Mass when the living and the dead are remembered. By extension this term may also be used to describe any intention or remembrance in prayer.

Memorare **(mem-oh-rahr-ray)**   Popular prayer to the Blessed Virgin Mary that began to be included in devotional books in the fifteenth century. Thought to be written by Saint Bernard of Clairvaux (d. 1153), it was actually popularized by Claude Bernard (d. 1641).

Morning Offering   Prayer said at the beginning of each day which offers all the "prayers, works, joys, and sufferings" of the day to God. This devotion was begun by a Father Gaurelet, a Jesuit, and was inspired by Christ's requests of Saint Margaret Mary Alacoque. The most common form of the Morning Offering is the one popularized by the Apostleship of Prayer.

Morning Prayer   Part of the Liturgy of the Hours prayed in the early morning at the beginning of another day. Morning Prayer, along with Evening Prayer, are the two "hinges" on which the daily prayer of the Church turns. Morning Prayer is structured to contain a hymn, two psalms (each psalm may be concluded by a prayer), an Old Testament canticle, a Scripture reading (which varies with the day) followed by a proper responsory; a short homily if Morning Prayer is celebrated with the faithful, followed by an optional period of silence; a solemn recitation of the Gospel Canticle of Zechariah followed by intercessions and consecration of the day and its work; finally, the Lord's Prayer is recited. A dismissal may complete the order if a priest or deacon is presiding. Morning Prayer may begin with the Invitatory Psalm, Psalm 95, if this is the first prayer period of the day.

Nicene Creed   Statement of Christian belief first formulated by the Council of Nicea in 325, and later affirmed and modified by the Council of Constantinople in 381. The creed is made up of three parts—one part treats of God the Father, one part treats of God the Son, and one part treats of God the Holy Spirit. Following these statements of belief are four affirmations that contradict the central precepts of the Arian heresy.

The bishops who wrote the Nicene Creed made two important additions to the text: they inserted "and the Son" after "we believe in the Holy Spirit, the Lord, the giver of life, who proceeds from the Father..."; and they made it clear through the words "true God from true God, begotten not made, one in Being with the Father" that the Son is equal in status with the Father.

None   Third of the three daytime hours of prayer, sometimes called "minor hours," and celebrated around 3:00 P.M. It is now called Midafternoon Prayer. The other two daytime hours are Midmorning (Terce) and Midday (Sext). According to the new revised format of the Liturgy of the Hours, only one of the three minor hours need be said (unless it is retained by a contemplative community as mandatory).

The new structure for Midafternoon Prayer is this: a verse and response ("O God, come to my assistance. O Lord, make haste to help me."); a hymn; three short psalms or three sections of a longer psalm; a passage from Scripture; verse, response, and collect; and, finally, the usual acclamations.

novena Devotion, either public or private, that is made up of a cycle of prayers repeated nine times. The prayers continue either for nine consecutive days (as in preparation for a special feast), for nine consecutive weeks (as nine Mondays), or nine consecutive months (as in the nine First Fridays). Novenas may be made for a particular intention, in honor of a particular saint, or a particular aspect of Christ (Sacred Heart) or the Blessed Virgin Mary (Our Lady of Perpetual Help).

Early novenas may have been based on the Roman custom of observing a nine-day period of sorrow and prayer after the death of a loved one or modeled after the apostles' nine days of prayer in the upper room.

O Antiphons Sequence of seven antiphons, each starting with the interjection "O," which are chanted before and after the Canticle of the Blessed Virgin Mary (the *Magnificat*) beginning with December 17. These prayer-texts are a loose mix of biblical verses from various books of the Bible. The O Antiphons are *O Sapientia* (Wisdom), *O Adonai* (Lord), *O Radix Jesse* (Root of Jesse), *O Clavis David* (Key of David), *O Oriens* (Radiant Dawn), *O Rex Gentium* (King of All Nations), and *O Emmanuel* (God-with-us).

Office of the Dead Variant of the Liturgy of the Hours used on November 2 (All Souls' Day) and sometimes, in whole or in part, as part of a funeral ceremony. At the beginning, it consisted of just the prayers for Matins, Lauds, and Vespers, but Pius X added the daytime sections. Reforms in 1971 made the Office of the Dead consistent in form with other offices. Some parts of the Office of the Dead are recommended in the 1970 Rite of Funerals.

orans (oh'-rans)   Term used for a human figure depicted with out-
stretched arms in the early Christian attitude of prayer. This figure is
drawn with his or her hands raised up, conveying a demeanor of praise
and adoration, with palms facing outward, and the elbows slightly
bent. The most famous *orans* is found in the fresco of the three praying
men in the Catacombs of Saint Priscilla in Rome.

Pater Noster   See **Lord's Prayer.**

Pax Christi   International peace organization of Catholics, formed in
1945, with centers in various countries. *Pax Christi* was originally
founded to seek reconciliation between French and German Catholics, especially through an exchange of prayers for peace. It soon became a crusade for peace among all nations.

Perpetual Adoration   Practice of maintaining continuous and uninterrupted adoration of the Blessed Sacrament, preferably with the consecrated host exposed on an altar, usually in a monstrance. Historically,
the practice of perpetual adoration is closely connected with Forty Hours
Devotion, although it was first brought to prominence by such medieval lay groups as the Beguines of Liège and the confraternities of the
Blessed Sacrament. Later, religious communities, such as the Congregation of Perpetual Adorers and the Nuns of the Perpetual Adoration
of the Blessed Sacrament, were founded with the main purpose of practicing continuous adoration of the Blessed Sacrament.

Recently the practice of perpetual adoration has gained renewed interest. Catholics are beginning to see that perpetual adoration is an
extremely effective means of focusing the heart and mind in prayer.

petition, prayer of   Fundamental request to God for the granting of
some human need or deliverance from some harm. Prayer of petition
is based on two seeming contradictions: God is a caring Father whom
we can "ask" and be confident that we will receive; and God is beyond
human control and so what we ask may not be granted. Thus, a prayer
of petition is not a series of specific requests, but a surrender of one's

needs and one's existence to the God who has already set the path of all creation. See also **intercession.**

prayers for the dead   Practice by the living of praying that God will admit the souls still in purgatory into heaven. This custom has been somewhat controversial, but verified by reference to 2 Maccabees 12:39–45 where Judas had sacrifices offered for the slain Jewish soldiers so that the sins they had committed "might be wholly blotted out," and by early Church writers, such as Clement of Alexandria, who recommended prayers for the dead. The basis for the practice of praying for the dead is the doctrine of the communion of saints: the living members of Christ's Body on earth can intercede for the deceased members of the Church who still must make atonement for sins before they may be admitted to heaven. Other ways the living may pray for the dead is through the liturgical observance of All Souls' Day on November 2 each year, through Masses of Christian Burial, by anniversary Masses for departed loved ones, and even small prayers uttered on the behalf of those who have preceded us in death.

presence, presence of God   Focus of prayer in which a person realizes, through love, that God is truly within the spirit of the one praying and is directing all of life's activity and all of creation. Human beings are present to God when they develop the gifts of the Holy Spirit by turning from their own egos to a faithful and attentive love of God. The Holy Spirit is in a special way the presence of God, the love that flows between the Father and Son.

Psalter   In the Middle Ages, a book containing the psalms used in the Divine Office (now the Liturgy of the Hours) and, later, that part of the Breviary containing psalms.

Quiet, Prayer of   Kind of contemplative prayer, a gift of God, in which the mind is enlightened and led to an interior peace and happiness in the presence of God. This form of prayer is a kind of contemplation and is usually only achieved after a life of virtue, and long practice of mediation. This term is one used by Saint Teresa of Ávila.

Raccolta Book containing prayers, devotions, and invocations to which the Church has granted indulgences. The first such collection was published originally in the early nineteenth century, but such books are now supplanted by other books.

recollection Term used by spiritual writers to describe an awareness of the presence of God. This inward attention involves alert focus on spiritual things so as to avoid distractions and activities that undermine the sense of God's inhabiting the soul.

Recollection curbs and moderates the details of ordinary living to maintain strength for the spiritual life. Silence, solitude, and prayer are aids to the practice of recollection.

retreat Period of time, varying in length, set aside for more intense spiritual work, usually in a place apart from the ordinary setting of daily life. A retreat can also refer to a place of tranquillity that fosters prayer and reflection.

Jesus Christ gave an example of a special time of prayer by his forty days in solitude in the desert (Mt 4:1–2). The apostles after the Ascension followed suit by spending time in continuous prayer in the upper room (Acts 1:12–14). And Paul, after his conversion, spent three days in fasting and solitude (Acts 9:9).

The concept of a retreat became more formalized with the introduction of the *Spiritual Exercises* of Saint Ignatius Loyola and the writings of Saint Francis de Sales, especially the *Introduction to the Devout Life.*

The retreat movement for lay people saw a blossoming in the late nineteenth century, fostered in the United States by national retreat leagues. Over five hundred retreat centers, many run by religious orders, are in existence in the U.S., offering programs of various lengths with varying spiritual goals. The daily retreat schedule is designed in many different ways, but common requirements may include a period of silence, a schedule of prayer, a series of talks, and conferences with a personal guide or retreat master.

Rosary String of beads on which is prayed the most common of Catholic devotions. Though legend attributes the origin of the rosary to Saint Dominic in the thirteenth century, its roots actually arise from several different sources, specifically as a memory aid for those who could not read the Psalms and instead substituted 150 Our Fathers for the 150 Psalms. The beads, as well as the Psalter, were often divided into sets of fifty.

As devotion to the Blessed Virgin increased, the Hail Mary (in its early form) was added to the Our Fathers, as well as the words of Elizabeth at Mary's visitation. Soon meditations on biblical events were added. Finally the Dominicans began preaching the rosary, popularizing it, founding rosary confraternities, and introducing many standardizations.

In modern times, the rosary is a devotion to the fifteen mysteries which are meditated on as each of the fifteen decades of the Hail Marys are recited. Each decade is followed by a Glory Be and preceded by an Our Father. Usually only one-third of the rosary is said at any one time.

Sign of the Cross Gesture that traces the outline of the Cross on people or things. It came into common use among the Christians of the second century as a private devotion to sanctify daily life and as a sign of mutual recognition during periods of persecution. Soon the sign was employed in the liturgy, in baptism, during the Mass, and as part of other blessings, and to the opening and closing of prayer. In the early Church, the sign of the Cross was customarily made by gesturing a small Cross on the forehead with the thumb. Later, a larger sign of the Cross came into use, wherein the hand moved from head to breast to shoulders.

This distinctive gesture is a symbol of a person's unity with Christ, an indication of status as a believer in the Cross as the central mystery of salvation, and a confirmation of baptism.

Stations of the Cross   Devotion honoring the passion and death of Christ, consisting of prayers and meditations on fourteen events experienced by Christ on his way to Calvary and his crucifixion. The practice probably originated with early pilgrims in the Holy Land, who processed from place to place in the city of Jerusalem, stopping at each point for prayer.

The devotion spread across Europe during the fifteenth century, largely because of the efforts of the Franciscans.

For many years, there existed a wide variety of stations, but the list became standard through a series of papal pronouncements. The following are the names of those stations observed in modern times: (1) Jesus is condemned to death; (2) Jesus carries his Cross; (3) Jesus falls the first time; (4) Jesus meets his Mother; (5) Simon of Cyrene helps Jesus carry his Cross; (6) Veronica wipes the face of Jesus; (7) Jesus falls the second time; (8) Jesus speaks to the women of Jerusalem; (9) Jesus falls the third time; (10) Jesus is stripped of his garments; (11) Jesus is nailed to the Cross; (12) Jesus dies on the Cross; (13) Jesus is taken down from the Cross; (14) Jesus is laid in the tomb.

Today the faithful make the "way of the Cross" alone or in a group with a prayer leader. When praying this devotion alone, a person may walk from one picture or symbol of a station of the Cross to another, meditating and praying in front of each one. In recent times, a final station—one depicting the Resurrection—has been added.

Vespers   Now known as Evening Prayer, Vespers is one of the two most important prayer times of the Liturgy of the Hours. Today Evening Prayer consists of the following: introductory verse, a hymn, two psalms and a New Testament canticle, with their antiphons, a reading from Scripture, a response, the *Magnificat* with antiphon, intercessions, the Lord's Prayer, a concluding prayer, and a final blessing.

Way of the Cross   See **Stations of the Cross**.